THE THREE COMINGS OF CHRIST

Daily Meditations for Advent

MIKE PACER

The Three Comings of Christ

DAILY MEDITATIONS FOR ADVENT

LIGHTHOUSE CATHOLIC PUBLISHING
SYCAMORE, ILLINOIS

Nihil Obstat: Ryan B. Browning, S.T.L.
Censor Liborum

Imprimatur: + David J. Malloy, D.D., J.C.L., S.T.D.
Bishop of Rockford

Cover art:
The Birth of Christ by Abraham Bloemaert
Jesus and the Passage to Emmaus by Gebhard Fugel
The Last Judgment by Jacob van Campen
Used by permission.

Cover design by Nathan McDevitt

CONTENTS

For my mother and father who led me on a beautiful Advent journey for so many years.

PREFACE

Advent — The Forgotten Season

The Christmas Season does not begin on "Black Friday." Rather, it begins after the Vigil Mass on Christmas Eve and continues until the Feast of the Baptism of Christ in early January. The four weeks leading up to Christmas (almost all of the time between Thanksgiving and Christmas) is the season of Advent.

At Christmas, we celebrate one event — the Birth of Christ. Given the importance of this event, we do not merely celebrate it for only one day but for two to three weeks. Advent is the commemoration of thousands of years — all of salvation history from creation until the Incarnation. Hence, it is important not to just skip Advent and head straight into Christmas. Even four weeks is not much time to commemorate thousands of years. More importantly, however, we need to live through Advent if we are to truly appreciate Christmas. In fact, Christmas makes no sense without Advent.

At Christmas, we celebrate the Incarnation, God coming as man. But why did God become man? Advent answers this question and provides the context necessary to understand the Incarnation. Therefore, celebrating Christmas without first observing Advent would be like giving birth without first being pregnant or receiving a trophy before running the race.

Salvation (Our) History

Salvation history refers to the time from creation to the Incarnation. The Old Testament is the divinely inspired recordation of this time. It is called "salvation" history because it is the story of our salvation — our being saved from all that separates us from God. It is the story of God creating us personally, out of love, to be in relationship with him, our turning away from him through sin, and his consistent invitation to return to him. It culminates in God sending his own Son to pay the price for our sin and open the gates of Heaven so that we might never be separated from God.

Salvation history is the history of the whole human race, but, more particularly, it is our own "family" history. It is the stories of the seminal moments in the lives of our ancestors. Some are direct physical ancestors (e.g., Adam, Eve, and Noah), but all are our spiritual ancestors who preceded us in entering into an ever-maturing relationship with God (e.g., Adam and Eve, Noah, Abraham, David, Mary, and Joseph). Just as we slowly come to know God better over the years of our lives, all of mankind slowly increased in its understanding of God as he gradually revealed himself over thousands of years. In prayerfully entering into salvation history (through reading and meditating upon the Old Testament), we come to know God through the way he revealed himself (but without having to wait thousands of years).

It is important to understand that the story of salvation history is a love story. It is the story of a God who is so much love that it cannot be contained. It must overflow to others. Hence, God created us to receive his love and live in his love. But man turned his back on God and ran away from his loving embrace. The result of this was suffering and death. Yet God loved his children so much that he wooed them back and forgave them when they returned to him. If only this were where the love story ended! But man left again, God wooed, man returned, and God forgave. And this happened again and again. God's ultimate act of love and forgiveness would be the culmination of this salvation history love story — God would send his own Son to become man, take upon himself all of the sins of mankind, and suffer and die for us … and then rise from the dead to open the way for our own resurrection and eternal embrace by God.

The Importance of Reading the Old Testament

It is easier to read the New Testament than the Old. The New Testament is more directly relevant in coming to know God and gaining in understanding of our purpose and how to live our lives. There is, however, an immeasurable wealth contained in the Old Testament. It contains thousands of years of God's messages to his people. It contains the words and deeds of so many holy men and women. It is (to an equal extent as the New Testament) the divinely revealed Word of God. And Jesus and his followers who authored the books of the New Testament constantly quoted from or made reference to passages of the Old Testament. In fact, the Old Testament points to the events recorded in the New Testament, and the New Testament fulfills what is foretold in the Old.

In reading the New Testament, we seek to appreciate who Jesus Christ is. In this regard, the Old Testament is the "paper" upon which the revelation of the New Testament is written. It is the foundation upon which the Church is built. It is the world into which and for which Christ was born. At Christmas, we seek to appreciate the coming of Christ as man. We cannot, however, fully appreciate the coming of Christ if we fail to understand the need for his coming and the longing that existed prior to his coming. No one more greatly appreciates water or better understands its importance than the person deprived of it for a long period of time. Or, to use a Christmas analogy, presents sitting under the tree for days before Christmas increase a child's joy in finally opening them on Christmas Day.

The "Three Comings of Christ"

We severely limit ourselves if Advent is merely a preparation for the commemoration of Christ's birth two thousand years ago. In doing so, we ignore our present and our future. We ignore the fact that Christ came two thousand years ago so that our "today" and our "tomorrow" would be radically different. In fact, the reason we commemorate the life of any historical figure is not just for what they did in the past but for how that affects us today — how our lives are changed because of what they accomplished and how they stood as examples of how we should live.

We can gain much by meditating every day in Advent upon the importance of the Incarnation. However, the great St. Bernard of Clairvaux challenges us to go further. St Bernard reminds us that there are really three comings of Christ. The First Coming of Christ was two thousand years ago when the second Person of the Blessed Trinity emptied himself of his divinity and was born as a baby in a stable in Bethlehem. The Second Coming of Christ is at the end of our lives — personally, Christ will come to us at our death; collectively, Christ will come to us all at the end of the world. We will be judged and enter into the eternity that we have chosen by way of our daily thoughts, words, and actions — an eternity with God ("Heaven"), perhaps after some purgation, or an eternity isolated from God ("Hell"). St. Bernard invites us to meditate upon this Second Coming and to keep Heaven as our constant goal. He also invites us to meditate upon a "Third Coming of Christ" — Christ's coming to us at every moment of every day, constantly asking us to let him into our hearts, constantly inviting us into a closer relationship of love with him. This book invites the reader to spend time in Advent meditating upon these three Comings of Christ in light of the seminal moments in salvation history. The reader is invited to walk along the path of salvation history and use that path as both a daily road map and a guide toward Heaven.

Mike Pacer
Solemnity of the Annunciation of the Lord

HOW TO USE THIS BOOK

There is no "right" or "wrong" way to use this book. It is merely a tool aimed at helping the reader journey closer to God during the season of Advent. It can be used by an individual or a group. The reader might, however, keep in mind that this book is not intended to be read cover to cover in a couple of sittings. It is meant to be slowly and prayerfully read daily over the first twenty-four days of December. Time should be allowed, if possible, for prayerful meditation upon the words of Scripture and the accompanying meditation. Scripture is most efficacious when it is not merely read but entered into and allowed to wash over the reader.

Individual Use

This book is intended to be used beginning on December 1 and ending on December 24. For each day, there is a Scripture passage. Accompanying each passage are three meditations. The first meditation for each day focuses on the First Coming of Christ — Christ's coming two thousand years ago as man. The second meditation focuses on the Second Coming of Christ — Christ's coming at the end of our lives. The third meditation focuses on the Third Coming of Christ — Christ's coming into our hearts personally each day.

You, the reader, must determine whether to use this book one or three times each day. If you can devote three separate times during the day to this spiritual journey, you could read the Scripture passage and first meditation in the morning, read the Scripture passage again and the second meditation during the day, and read the Scripture passage and the third meditation at night. Another recommended option is to read the third meditation (Christ's coming to us at every moment of every day) during the day when you are actively meeting Christ through the events of your day-to-day life, and the second meditation (Christ's coming to us at our death and his coming at the end of the world) as part of your night prayer. If you only have time for one meditation per day, you might consider embarking upon this spiritual journey for three Advents in a row, focusing on one set of meditations each year.

Use of the Biblical Passages as Family Prayer during Advent

It would be a wonderful Advent practice for a family to read the stories of salvation history together each night. Family nighttime prayers can be substituted for the meditation. It would be great to begin this tradition when the children are young and, as they grow, allow them to take turns reading the Scripture passage for the day. It would be nice to do this in the presence of an Advent Wreath. Another possible addition would be the singing of one verse of an Advent song prior to reading the passage and prayers (e.g., "O Come, O Come, Emmanuel," "The King of Glory Comes," "People Look East," or other well-known Advent songs).

DECEMBER 1

Reading: The Story of Creation[1]

In the beginning God created the heavens and the earth. The earth was without form and void, and darkness was upon the face of the deep; and the Spirit of God was moving over the face of the waters.

And God said, "Let there be light"; and there was light. And God saw that the light was good; and God separated the light from the darkness. God called the light Day, and the darkness he called Night. And there was evening and there was morning, one day.

And God said, "Let there be a firmament in the midst of the waters, and let it separate the waters from the waters." . . . And God called the firmament Heaven. And there was evening and there was morning, a second day.

And God said, "Let the waters under the heavens be gathered together into one place, and let the dry land appear." . . . God called the dry land Earth, and the waters that were gathered together he called Seas. And God saw that it was good. And God said, "Let the earth put forth vegetation, plants yielding seed, and fruit trees bearing fruit in which is their seed, each according to its kind, upon the earth." And it was so. The earth brought forth vegetation. . . . And God saw that it was good. And there was evening and there was morning, a third day.

And God said, "Let there be lights in the firmament of the heavens to separate the day from the night; and let them be for signs and for seasons and for days and years, and let them be lights

[1] Genesis 1:1–6, 8–16, 18–31; 2:1–3.

in the firmament of the heavens to give light upon the earth." . . . And God made the two great lights, the greater light to rule the day, and the lesser light to rule the night; he made the stars also. . . . And God saw that it was good. And there was evening and there was morning, a fourth day.

And God said, "Let the waters bring forth swarms of living creatures, and let birds fly above the earth across the firmament of the heavens." . . . And God saw that it was good. And God blessed them, saying, "Be fruitful and multiply and fill the waters in the seas, and let birds multiply on the earth." And there was evening and there was morning, a fifth day.

And God said, "Let the earth bring forth living creatures according to their kinds: cattle and creeping things and beasts of the earth according to their kinds." . . . And God saw that it was good.

Then God said, "Let us make man in our image, after our likeness; and let them have do-minion over the fish of the sea, and over the birds of the air, and over the cattle, and over all the earth, and over every creeping thing that creeps upon the earth." So God created man in his own image, in the image of God he created him; male and female he created them. And God blessed them, and God said to them, "Be fruitful and multiply, and fill the earth and subdue it; and have dominion over the fish of the sea and over the birds of the air and over every living thing that moves upon the earth." And God said, "Behold, I have given you every plant yielding seed which is upon the face of all the earth, and every tree with seed in its fruit; you shall have them for food. And to every beast of the earth, and to every bird of the air, and to everything that creeps on the earth, everything that has the breath of life, I have given every green plant for food." And it was so. And God saw everything that he had made, and behold, it was very good. And there was evening and there was morning, a sixth day.

Thus the heavens and the earth were finished, and all the host of them. And on the seventh day God finished his work which he had done, and he rested on the seventh day from all his work which he had done. So God blessed the seventh day and hallowed it, because on it God rested from all his work which he had done in creation.

Meditation 1: The First Coming of Christ

In the creation narrative, we see great order and purpose in God's activity. First, he created the physical world in which man could live — light, physical substance, and water; then plants and animals for man to eat — and then man himself. But man is not the pinnacle of creation. For man, as created by God, was only made in the image and likeness of God and was not God himself. One day, creation would see its consummation in the Incarnation of God as man in the Person of Jesus Christ.

The existence of the Son (as well as the Holy Spirit) is hinted at in the words "let us make man in our image" (Gn 1:26; emphasis added). This is confirmed in the words of the Gospel of John: "In the beginning was the Word, and the Word was with God, and the Word was God. He was in the beginning with God; all things came to be through him, and without him was not anything made that was made. In him was life, and the life was the light of men" (Jn 1:1–4).

When we read these two passages together, we see the future coming of the Son revealed in creation. The Father created the world through the Son, and the Son would be the world's source of light and life.

The sun and moon would not ultimately be our sources of illumination. Rather, the Son himself would be our true light, revealing the Father to us and revealing our true identities as beloved children of the Father. The Son would come one day as man, like us in all things but sin. He would take on our mortal flesh and perfect it. He would teach us to call God "Father." He would reveal the love of the Father for us his children.

The original life breathed into us was subject to the possibility of physical death. Because of man's sin, death would enter into the world, and man would die. The Son would come to be the source of true never-ending life. The Son would come to save us from death and to open the gates of eternal life.

It is the supreme meditation of the loving humility of God to reflect upon the fact that the Creator of the universe would choose to one day enter into that physical creation and be born as a little baby in a manger two thousand years ago.

Meditation 2: The Second Coming of Christ

"In the beginning . . ." God, who is eternal, has no beginning and no end. All time is "now" for him. But we who are created by God have a beginning — a time when our souls were willed into existence by God and united to a physical body. As mortal beings, we also have an end. A day will come when our current existence will end, and a new one will begin.

There are really two ends to which we look forward. Most of mankind will experience a physical death in the natural order of things. We will die, be judged, and end up in one of three states of existence: (1) Heaven — eternal union with God; (2) Purgatory — a state in which we will be purified and made able to enter into Heaven; or (3) Hell — complete, eternal isolation from God. At some point, however, the entire universe will come to an end, all mankind will be judged, and the fullness of creation (Heaven) will begin.

The "end" is the Second Coming of Christ. Whether at the end of our lives or at the end of time, Christ will come to us individually and personally. We must keep this Second Coming of

Christ in mind always. What will happen when Christ comes? Will he find you ready to receive him? Will you have lived a life of love for him and his Father? Will he welcome you into Heaven? What must you do to prepare for this Second Coming?

Meditation 3: The Third Coming of Christ

The story of creation is meant to teach us how much God loves us and that he invites us to respond to that love.

God did not need to create us. There was nothing lacking in God that he sought to fulfill through our creation. God is Trinity — Father, Son, and Holy Spirit — a perfect unity of persons, a perfect "family," loving, receiving love, and returning that perfect love. Yet God is so much love that he desired to create us in order that we might also receive his love. God created us because he loved us for all eternity, even before we were physically brought into being. God created us to receive his love and to be free to love him in return. We are created by God in love. We are created by God to receive his love. And we are created by God with the ability to love him in return.

God created the entire universe for us — the sun, the moon, and the stars, unfathomable numbers of planets and other celestial bodies, the wind, the earth, and the plants and animals. Everything that exists in the created universe was created by God for us. Everything exists for us. What an awesome, magnanimous, loving God we have!

Unlike any other creature, we are created in the very image and likeness of God. We possess immortal, sentient souls. We, alone of all God's creatures, are called to live in intentional relationship with God. We have been given the freedom to receive God's love and to love God in return.

Let us cooperate in God's plan of creation that we would receive his love and life. How can you embrace your role as a beloved son or daughter of the Father? How can you invite God into your heart in a new and deeper way this Advent?

DECEMBER 2

Reading: Expulsion from Eden[1]

Now the serpent was more subtle than any other wild creature that the LORD God had made. He said to the woman, "Did God say, 'You shall not eat of any tree of the garden'?" And the woman said to the serpent, "We may eat of the fruit of the trees of the garden; but God said, 'You shall not eat of the fruit of the tree which is in the midst of the garden, neither shall you touch it, lest you die.'" But the serpent said to the woman, "You will not die. For God knows that when you eat of it your eyes will be opened, and you will be like God, knowing good and evil." So when the woman saw that the tree was good for food, and that it was a delight to the eyes, and that the tree was to be desired to make one wise, she took of its fruit and ate; and she also gave some to her husband, and he ate. Then the eyes of both were opened, and they knew that they were naked; and they sewed fig leaves together and made themselves aprons.

And they heard the sound of the LORD God walking in the garden in the cool of the day, and the man and his wife hid themselves from the presence of the LORD God among the trees of the garden. But the LORD God called to the man, and said to him, "Where are you?" And he said, "I heard the sound of you in the garden, and I was afraid, because I was naked; and I hid myself." He said, "Who told you that you were naked? Have you eaten of the tree of which I commanded you not to eat?" The man said, "The woman whom you gave to be with me, she gave me fruit

[1] Genesis 3:1–21, 23–24.

of the tree, and I ate." Then the LORD God said to the woman,
"What is this that you have done?" The woman said, "The serpent beguiled me, and I ate." The LORD God said to the serpent,

"Because you have done this,
    cursed are you above all cattle,
    and above all wild animals;
upon your belly you shall go,
    and dust you shall eat
    all the days of your life.
I will put enmity between you and the woman,
    and between your seed and her seed;
he shall bruise your head,
    and you shall bruise his heel."
To the woman he said,
    "I will greatly multiply your pain in childbearing;
        in pain you shall bring forth children,
    yet your desire shall be for your husband,
        and he shall rule over you."
And to Adam he said,
    "Because you have listened to the voice of your wife,
        and have eaten of the tree
    of which I commanded you,
        'You shall not eat of it,'
    cursed is the ground because of you;
        in toil you shall eat of it all the days of your life;
    thorns and thistles it shall bring forth to you;
        and you shall eat the plants of the field.
    In the sweat of your face
        you shall eat bread
    till you return to the ground,
        for out of it you were taken;
    you are dust,
        and to dust you shall return."

The man called his wife's name Eve, because she was the mother of all living. And the LORD God made for Adam and for his wife garments of skins, and clothed them. . . .

Therefore the LORD God sent him forth from the garden of Eden, to till the ground from which he was taken. He drove out the man; and at the east of the garden of Eden he placed the cherubim, and a flaming sword which turned every way, to guard the way to the tree of life.

Meditation 1: The First Coming of Christ

Hidden within the account of the Fall of Man is an incredibly joyful statement that foretells the First Coming of Christ: "I will put enmity between you and the woman, and between your seed and her seed; he shall bruise your head, and you shall bruise his heel" (Gn 3:15). This passage is referred to as the "protoevangeli-um" (from the Greek word for "first gospel") because it is the first announcement of the Good News of salvation. It announces the coming of the Messiah — the "seed of the woman" — who will destroy the devil and all his progeny.

When we combine yesterday's reading (on creation) with to-day's, we see the full Gospel message: God created us in love to live in perfect harmony with him, we separated ourselves from God because of our sin, and God would send his own Son to destroy the effects of that sin and open the gates to the perfect Eden — eternal joy with God in Heaven.

How amazing is it that, immediately after man sinned and received the consequences, God announced he would "fix every-thing." But God went even further than that: He promised not merely to restore things to the way they were in Eden but to make things infinitely better. God would send his Son to be born as man in a stable in Bethlehem. Through Christ's life, death, and Resurrection, our Lord would not merely reopen the gate to Eden but to Heaven. We would not just walk in the garden with God, like Adam and Eve, but be perfectly united to him forever as his own children. It is this reality that is proclaimed at the Easter Vigil Mass every year: "O happy fault that earned so great, so glorious a Redeemer!"[2]

Meditation 2: The Second Coming of Christ

The story of the Fall of man invites us to meditate upon the Second Coming of Christ. Adam and Eve are not the only two sinners to walk this earth. Each one of us is a sinner. As St. Paul states, "All have sinned and fall short of the glory of God" (Rm 3:23). Christ will come again to each of us personally at our death and call us to account for our lives.

Jesus is both just and merciful. We will be held accountable for all of our thoughts, words, and actions that have separated us from God. In justice, if while on earth we have chosen to separate ourselves from God, he will allow that separation to be complete and eternal in Hell. In mercy, however, if we have generally tried to live with God and walk in his ways while here on earth, or at least were truly contrite for our sins at the time of our death, God will forgive our sins and allow us to be with him forever in Heaven (although some purification in Purgatory might be necessary).

We cannot earn our way into Heaven. Fortunately, we do not have to. God is so infinitely merciful that there is no sin that he is unwilling to forgive. He will not withhold his mercy from anyone who asks for it. Are you preparing for Christ's Second Coming by seeking to love him and constantly asking for his great mercy?

---

[2] *Roman Missal*, The Easter Vigil in the Holy Night, "The Easter Proclamation."

Meditation 3: The Third Coming of Christ

This story points out that God came to Adam and Eve in the garden, but, in their shame, they were afraid and hid themselves from him. God called out, "Where are you?" (Gn 3:9).

Christ comes to you today. He looks for you. He calls out to you personally, "Where are you?" Have you hidden yourself from him by making choices that separate you from him? Are you "naked" and "ashamed?" How will you respond to Christ's call?

Christ wants only one response from you: "Here I am Lord!" (1 Sm 3:4). It doesn't matter what you have done. It doesn't matter how far you have distanced yourself from God. It doesn't matter if you are completely "naked" in the shame of grave sin. If you but call out to Christ, he will come to you. He will offer you the cloak of his infinite mercy.

When he comes to you, do not make excuses. Do not blame others. Merely say, "I am sorry." Christ will clothe you and bring you back to the Father. Are you ready to respond when he calls?

DECEMBER 3

Reading: Noah and the Ark[1]

The LORD saw that the wickedness of man was great in the earth, and that every imagination of the thoughts of his heart was only evil continually. And the LORD was sorry that he had made man on the earth, and it grieved him to his heart. So the LORD said, "I will blot out man whom I have created from the face of the ground, man and beast and creeping things and birds of the air, for I am sorry that I have made them." But Noah found favor in the eyes of the LORD. . . .

And God said to Noah, "I have determined to make an end of all flesh; for the earth is filled with violence through them; behold, I will destroy them with the earth. Make yourself an ark of gopher wood; make rooms in the ark, and cover it inside and out with pitch. This is how you are to make it: the length of the ark three hundred cubits, its breadth fifty cubits, and its height thirty cubits. Make a roof for the ark, and finish it to a cubit above; and set the door of the ark in its side; make it with lower, second, and third decks. For behold, I will bring a flood of waters upon the earth, to destroy all flesh in which is the breath of life from under heaven; everything that is on the earth shall die. But I will establish my covenant with you; and you shall come into the ark, you, your sons, your wife, and your sons' wives with you. And of every living thing of all flesh, you shall bring two of every sort into the ark, to keep them alive with you. . . . Noah . . . did all that God commanded him. . . .

[1] Genesis 6:5–8, 13–19, 22; 7:11–16.

In the six hundredth year of Noah's life, in the second month, on the seventeenth day of the month, on that day all the fountains of the great deep burst forth, and the windows of the heavens were opened. And rain fell upon the earth forty days and forty nights. On the very same day Noah and his sons, Shem and Ham and Ja pheth, and Noah's wife and the three wives of his sons with them entered the ark, they and every beast according to its kind, and all the cattle according to their kinds, and every creeping thing that creeps on the earth according to its kind, and every bird according to its kind, every bird of every sort. They went into the ark with Noah, two and two of all flesh in which there was the breath of life. And they that entered, male and female of all flesh, went in as God had commanded him; and the LORD shut him in.

Meditation 1: The First Coming of Christ

Noah is a "type" of Christ — that is, he foreshadows Christ. The lives of Noah and other key figures in the Old Testament reveal important aspects of the Messiah, Jesus Christ, who will come into the world at a later date. What they foreshadow, Christ will complete.

Around the time of Noah, wickedness abounded in human beings, and in their hearts was "only evil" (Gn 6:5). Noah, however, was a good man who found favor with the Lord. And, because of Noah, God decided not to destroy all of creation. Through Noah, mankind was saved and given another chance.

At Christmas, we celebrate the coming of the ultimate "good man," Jesus Christ — true God yet also true man. Two thousand years ago, Jesus came not merely to save mankind from the physical destruction of a flood but from the eternal destruction of sin. And Noah played a role in making God's salvation available to future generations. Christ personally empowers and offers salvation to all mankind — from Adam and Eve to the last child born before the end of the world.

Meditation 2: The Second Coming of Christ

At first blush, the story of the Flood can seem rather harsh. God might be thought cruel in his desire to destroy all mankind and all of creation. But to think this is to miss the point of the story. God would have been completely justified in destroying mankind. This passage is very clear — the hearts of all men, at the time of Noah, were turned completely to evil. And even Noah, who found favor with God, was, of course, not perfect.

When we think of Christ coming at the end of time, we might have a tendency to see him as the vengeful judge who is going to try his people and condemn many of them. It is true that Christ will come and judge us all. But, just as Christ will come with judgment, he will come with mercy as well.

God did not destroy creation. He spared it. God gave Noah the formula for the ark through which he and his family might be saved. Christ has given us the "ark" of the Church, containing his teachings and sacraments by which we might be saved. As God desired to spare Noah and his family from destruction, he desires to spare us. Will you choose to live in fear of God's judgment or embrace his mercy?

Meditation 3: The Third Coming of Christ

What waters are rising up in your life? What is your cause for despair? What destruction do you currently face? What are your fears?

The waters of the Flood foreshadow Christian Baptism. Through Baptism, you passed through death to life. You were cleansed of Original Sin and adopted as a child of God. Because you were baptized, you have become the very brother or sister of Christ. But Baptism alone is not enough to see you to your destination of Heaven. Every day, you must navigate the waves of temptation and despair. To do so, you need to stay close to Christ.

Christ comes to you personally today and, like Noah, finds you worthy and favorable. Christ wants to save you from all that separates you from him. He wants to bring you safely through the raging waters that are rising around you. Christ offers you salvation. He offers to be your ark. But you must trust him and get in the boat.

DECEMBER 4

Reading: Covenant with Noah[1]

In the six hundred and first year, in the first month, the first day of the month, the waters were dried from off the earth; and Noah removed the covering of the ark, and looked, and behold, the face of the ground was dry. . . . Then God said to Noah, "Go forth from the ark, you and your wife, and your sons and your sons' wives with you. Bring forth with you every living thing that is with you of all flesh — birds and animals and every creeping thing that creeps on the earth — that they may breed abundantly on the earth, and be fruitful and multiply upon the earth." So Noah went forth, and his sons and his wife and his sons' wives with him. And every beast, every creeping thing, and every bird, everything that moves upon the earth, went forth by families out of the ark.

Then Noah built an altar to the LORD, and took of every clean animal and of every clean bird, and offered burnt offerings on the altar. And when the LORD smelled the pleasing odor, the LORD said in his heart, "I will never again curse the ground because of man, for the imagination of man's heart is evil from his youth; neither will I ever again destroy every living creature as I have done. . . .

And God blessed Noah and his sons, and said to them, "Be fruitful and multiply, and fill the earth. The fear of you and the dread of you shall be upon every beast of the earth, and upon every bird of the air, upon everything that creeps on the ground and all the fish of the sea; into your hand they are delivered. Every

---

[1] Genesis 8:13, 15–21; 9:1–3, 8–9, 11–15.

moving thing that lives shall be food for you; and as I gave you the green plants, I give you everything. . . .

Then God said to Noah and to his sons with him, "Behold, I establish my covenant with you and your descendants after you . . . that never again shall all flesh be cut off by the waters of a flood, and never again shall there be a flood to destroy the earth." And God said, "This is the sign of the covenant which I make between me and you and every living creature that is with you, for all future generations: I set my bow in the cloud, and it shall be a sign of the covenant between me and the earth. When I bring clouds over the earth and the bow is seen in the clouds, I will remember my covenant which is between me and you; and the waters shall never again become a flood to destroy all flesh.

Meditation 1: The First Coming of Christ

This is a story of a "second creation." It mirrors the first but is not identical. In both stories, the waters recede to bring forth vegetation. In both stories, the earth is populated with animals. In both stories, man is to "be fruitful and multiply, and fill the earth" (Gn 1:28; 9:1). However, at the point of the first creation, man was to "have dominion over" all of creation (Gn 1:28). In this second account, all creation is in fear and dread of man (see Gn 9:2).

The first dominion was harmonious — man in his rightful place, working with God as the pinnacle of creation. The second is after the Fall of man and the introduction of sin. This second creation finds man stained by Original Sin and bearing its effects. Man's will is no longer in alignment with God's. He does not co-operate with nature but subjugates it to fulfill his desires. In this passage, God remarks that the desires of the human heart are evil from youth. As we would see if we read on in Genesis, Noah and his family are far from perfect.

Despite mankind's sinfulness, God makes a covenant with mankind through Noah. God will never utterly destroy the world. While we can take this as a literal promise, the implied promise is far more important. God promises not merely the avoidance of destruction but ultimate and perfect salvation. One day, the true ark will come and deliver mankind from the waters of death. Jesus, the Savior, will come and institute the Sacrament of Baptism. Waters will no longer destroy man for his sin. It will wash him of sin. Through Jesus, water will not merely transport mankind to dry land where he may live out his days. Rather, it will change his very nature, transforming him into an adopted son of God.

Meditation 2: The Second Coming of Christ

We can often get caught up in the here and now. We can be lulled into a sense of "this is all there is." This makes us lose sight of the reality that, as St. Paul says, "here we have no lasting city, but we seek the city which is to come" (Heb 13:14). This earthly life around us is not all there is. There is much more. We are merely passing through on our way to our final destination — Heaven.

This story of Noah after the Flood makes it clear that the world is not how God intends it. It is not the perfection that God desires for us. In fact, it is not even as good as it was in the Garden of Eden. The time in the ark was literally a respite from the torrents of the waves and figuratively a respite from the torrents of sin and death. We can look to the ark as a bridge between Eden and Heaven. Noah and his family are at peace with creation — all of the animals and mankind live together in harmony under the protection of God.

The covenant with Noah following the Flood is a foreshadowing of the Second Coming of Christ, who will come and take us from the sin and pain of our current life to a new and glorious future existence. What distractions of the world are keeping you from focusing on the eternal destination that awaits you?

Meditation 3: The Third Coming of Christ

This is a story of a second chance. Man fails. God comes to man and offers him another chance. He offers man new life and a new relationship with him. This is the on-going, everyday story of our lives.

Today (and every day), Jesus comes to you personally. He wants to forgive you for your past sins, for the times you have turned (or run) away from him. He wants to wash you clean in the water that flowed from his side on the Cross. He wants to renew his Father's covenant with you — to be your Father and for you to be his own son or daughter.

God loves you just as you are, despite your sins and failings. He wants to give you life in abundance — the life that is found in the very love of the Trinity.

Are you lost and do not know where you are going? Ask Jesus to come and guide you. Are the waters of fear and despair rising up around you? Ask Jesus to carry you to safety. Are you ashamed of your sin? Ask Jesus to wash you and make you clean.

DECEMBER 5

Reading: Abraham — Call and Covenant[1]

Now the LORD said to Abram, "Go from your country and your kindred and your father's house to the land that I will show you. And I will make of you a great nation, and I will bless you, and make your name great, so that you will be a blessing. I will bless those who bless you, and him who curses you I will curse; and by you all the families of the earth shall bless themselves."

So Abram went, as the LORD had told him; and Lot went with him. Abram was seventy-five years old when he departed from Haran. . . .

After these things the word of the LORD came to Abram in a vision, "Fear not, Abram, I am your shield; your reward shall be very great." But Abram said, "O Lord GOD, what will you give me, for I continue childless, and the heir of my house is Elie'zer of Damascus?" And Abram said, "Behold, you have given me no off-spring; and a slave born in my house will be my heir." And behold, the word of the LORD came to him, "This man shall not be your heir; your own son shall be your heir." And he brought him out-side and said, "Look toward heaven, and number the stars, if you are able to number them." Then he said to him, "So shall your descendants be." And he believed the LORD; and he reckoned it to him as righteousness. . . .

When Abram was ninety-nine years old the LORD appeared to Abram, and said to him, "I am God Almighty; walk before me, and be blameless. And I will make my covenant between me and

[1] Genesis 12:1–4; 15:1–6; 17:1–8.

you, and will multiply you exceedingly." Then Abram fell on his face; and God said to him, "Behold, my covenant is with you, and you shall be the father of a multitude of nations. No longer shall your name be Abram, but your name shall be Abraham; for I have made you the father of a multitude of nations. I will make you exceedingly fruitful; and I will make nations of you, and kings shall come forth from you. And I will establish my covenant between me and you and your descendants after you throughout their generations for an everlasting covenant, to be God to you and to your descendants after you. And I will give to you, and to your descendants after you, the land of your sojournings, all the land of Canaan, for an everlasting possession; and I will be their God."

Meditation 1: The First Coming of Christ

Above all things, Abraham wanted to have an heir. He was willing to leave everything he knew at the promise that God would "make of [him] a great nation" (Gn 12:2). Yet God promised much more. He promised Abraham that he would be the father of a multitude of nations, that kings would stem from him, and that his descendants would be countless.

This promise must have thrilled Abraham. But it also undoubtedly seemed too good to be true. Not just an heir was promised but uncountable heirs. He would not just be the father of a clan or tribe but of nations ruled by kings! Yet the gift of God was even greater than this. From Abraham would come the King of Kings, the Messiah, God's own Son, Jesus Christ!

Meditation 2: The Second Coming of Christ

In making an everlasting covenant with Abraham, God draws our attention to the Second Coming of Christ. No "everlasting" covenant can occur in this world. This world is coming to an end. The law of entropy makes this abundantly clear. Everything around us is slowly fading away. Our own lives remind us that everything is working toward an end . . . and a new beginning.

God's everlasting covenant with us is not merely the land of Canaan or even the whole world as it exists now. It is not merely a promise of a good, long life. It is not merely the promise of future generations. God's everlasting covenant is the promise of a glorious eternity in Heaven with him. Whenever we feel the pain of this world, we must remind ourselves that we have a wonderful future to look forward to. Do you trust in God's promise that he will come to you personally, heal you, and take you to your eternal home? Come, Lord Jesus. Come!

Meditation 3: The Third Coming of Christ

Christ wants to be intimately involved in your life. But he does not always approach you in the way you would expect. God asked Abraham to leave all he knew — his home, his land, and his family — and go to a place he had never been. God promised Abraham that he would bless him with descendants more count-less than the stars in the sky, even though Abraham and his wife Sarah were beyond child-bearing age. God required Abraham to trust him completely.

Christ wants to bless you abundantly, just as he blessed Abra-ham. He wants to bestow upon you the miraculous, just as he did for Abraham. But, as he did with Abraham, he asks you to trust him . . . completely.

Jesus never forced any miracle upon anyone. He never cured anyone who did not seek a cure. He did not forgive the sins of any-one who failed to seek forgiveness. While he applauded great faith, he rewarded even the slightest. If you have any question of this, merely reflect upon the dialogue between Jesus and the Father of the possessed boy who struggled to believe that Jesus could heal his son and cried out, "I do believe, help my unbelief!" (Mk 9:20–27).

Jesus comes to you today and invites you to leave behind your old way of life, to follow him to a new and glorious destination. You do not need to know what will happen or where you will end. You do not have to have the greatest faith or trust. You need merely say a meek yes and follow him. What are you holding on to that Jesus is asking you to release? Do you trust that he will take care of you?

DECEMBER 6

Reading: Abraham and Isaac[1]

Sarah conceived, and bore Abraham a son in his old age at the time of which God had spoken to him. Abraham called the name of his son who was born to him, whom Sarah bore him, Isaac. And Abraham circumcised his son Isaac when he was eight days old, as God had commanded him. Abraham was a hundred years old when his son Isaac was born to him. . . .

God tested Abraham, and said to him, "Abraham!" And he said, "Here am I." He said, "Take your son, your only-begotten son Isaac, whom you love, and go to the land of Mori'ah, and offer him there as a burnt offering upon one of the mountains of which I shall tell you." So Abraham rose early in the morning, saddled his donkey, and took two of his young men with him, and his son Isaac; and he cut the wood for the burnt offering, and arose and went to the place of which God had told him. On the third day Abraham lifted up his eyes and saw the place afar off. Then Abraham said to his young men, "Stay here with the donkey; I and the lad will go yonder and worship, and come again to you." And Abraham took the wood of the burnt offering, and laid it on Isaac his son; and he took in his hand the fire and the knife. So they went both of them together. And Isaac said to his father Abraham, "My father!" And he said, "Here am I, my son." He said, "Behold, the fire and the wood; but where is the lamb for a burnt offering?" Abraham said, "God will provide himself the lamb for a burnt offering, my son." So they went both of them together.

[1] Genesis 21:2–5; 22:1–18.

When they came to the place of which God had told him, Abraham built an altar there, and laid the wood in order, and bound Isaac his son, and laid him on the altar, upon the wood. Then Abraham put forth his hand, and took the knife to slay his son. But the angel of the LORD called to him from heaven, and said, "Abraham, Abraham!" And he said, "Here am I." He said, "Do not lay your hand on the lad or do anything to him; for now I know that you fear God, seeing you have not with-held your son, your only-begotten son, from me." And Abraham lifted up his eyes and looked, and behold, behind him was a ram, caught in a thicket by his horns; and Abraham went and took the ram, and offered it up as a burnt offering instead of his son. So Abraham called the name of that place The LORD will provide; as it is said to this day, "On the mount of the LORD it shall be provided."

And the angel of the LORD called to Abraham a second time from heaven, and said, "By myself I have sworn, says the LORD, because you have done this, and have not withheld your son, your only-begotten son, I will indeed bless you, and I will multiply your descendants as the stars of heaven and as the sand which is on the seashore. And your descendants shall possess the gate of their enemies, and by your descendants shall all the nations of the earth bless themselves, because you have obeyed my voice."

Meditation 1: The First Coming of Christ

There is perhaps no other passage in the Old Testament that so overtly points to the coming of Jesus the Messiah. God tested the willingness of Abraham to sacrifice his only son yet did not require it of him. Conversely, the Father sent his only Son to be sacrificed on Calvary for all of us. Isaac was made to carry the wood (the instrument for the immolation of the sacrifice) on his shoulders. Jesus was made to carry the wood of the Cross on which he would be crucified. Isaac marched toward the place of sacrifice as directed by his father. Jesus marched toward Calvary in perfect obedience to his Father.

Abraham was inspired to answer Isaac's inquiry with the words, "God will provide himself the lamb for a burnt offering" (Gn 22:8). At that time, God sent a ram to be sacrificed. Later, God would send a lamb — Jesus, the "Lamb of God" (Jn 1:29) — to be the one perfect sacrifice for all times.

Abraham could not see exactly how God would fulfill his promise to make him the father of many nations after the death of his son Isaac. Presumably, Abraham trusted that God would send him and Sarah another son. Likewise, it was unfathomable to the Jews, Jesus' Apostles, and the whole world how, through the seemingly ignominious death of Jesus of Nazareth, the entire world would be saved from sin and recreated in God's image.

Meditation 2: The Second Coming of Christ

The blood of the Lamb, Jesus Christ, was literally poured out in sacrifice for our sins at a specific time. But this sacrifice was an eternal act that extended back to the beginning, expiating the sins of all mankind since the time of Adam and Eve. This sacrifice also extends forward to the end of time. The lamb of sacrifice alluded to in this passage is the same "Lamb" referred to in the Book of Revelation. Jesus, the Lamb of God, will come again at the end of time to bring his sacrifice on Calvary to a conclusion.

In chapter 21 of Revelation, we see that he will "make all things new" at the end of time (Rev 21:5). The bride of the Lamb — the New Jerusalem (the Church purified by the blood of the Lamb) — will descend from Heaven; that is, in Christ, we will be purified and recreated in our resurrected bodies. There will be no need to go to the Temple to worship. The Lamb will be our Temple. We will be so closely united to God that our very existence will be a constant worship of God.

For Abraham, the coming of the true Lamb may have seemed a long time away. In fact, two thousand years passed from Abraham to the coming of the Lamb at the Incarnation, and two thousand years have passed since the sacrifice of the Lamb on Calvary. Yet the last passages of Revelation assure us that Christ is coming "soon" (Rev 22:12) and admonish us to pray for that coming — "Come, Lord Jesus!" (Rev 22:20). Is this the daily prayer of your heart?

Meditation 3: The Third Coming of Christ

Jesus wishes to come into our lives every day. However, he does not necessarily approach in the way we would prefer but does so in the way that is best for us. Often, Jesus comes and asks of us something that seems very difficult or distasteful. But Jesus never asks anything of us that is not in our best interest. Nor will he ever fail to give us the strength we need to accomplish what he asks if we cooperate with him. Further, the result of our cooperation with the divine will always bring about a good that we cannot fully comprehend.

Abraham did not want to sacrifice his son. But he trusted in God and was blessed abundantly for his yes. In his Letter to the Romans, St. Paul encourages us to have that same faith. He points out that just as Abraham was righteous in the eyes of the Lord for his faith, we, too, will share in Abraham's righteousness, if we share in his faith. For us, this is faith in the death and Resurrection of Jesus. We must assent to this reality and act accordingly.

Each of us will be called to sacrifice things for Christ. Each of us will be called to bear witness to Christ at an uncomfortable time. Each of us is invited to walk daily with Christ along a path that varies in its difficulty. And each of us is promised an eternal love affair with Christ that begins, not at the end of our lives, but at this very moment. Are you afraid to follow Christ where he leads? Why do you not trust that he who sacrificed everything for you will bless you abundantly?

Jesus comes to you today and invites you to leave behind your old way of life, to follow him to a new and glorious destination. You do not need to know what will happen or where you will end. You do not have to have the greatest faith or trust. You need merely say a meek yes and follow him. What are you holding on to that Jesus is asking you to release? Do you trust that he will take care of you?

DECEMBER 7

Reading: Jacob — Birth and Blessing[1]

Isaac was forty years old when he took to wife Rebekah. . . . And Isaac prayed to the LORD for his wife, because she was barren; and the LORD granted his prayer, and Rebekah his wife conceived. The children struggled together within her; and she said, "If it is thus, why do I live?" So she went to inquire of the LORD. And the LORD said to her,

"Two nations are in your womb,

and two peoples, born of you, shall be divided

the one shall be stronger than the other,

the elder shall serve the younger."

When her days to be delivered were fulfilled, behold, there were twins in her womb. The first came forth red, all his body like a hairy mantle; so they called his name Esau. Afterward his brother came forth, and his hand had taken hold of Esau's heel; so his name was called Jacob. . . .

When the boys grew up, Esau was a skillful hunter, a man of the field, while Jacob was a quiet man, dwelling in tents. Isaac loved Esau, because he ate of his game; but Rebekah loved Jacob.

Once when Jacob was boiling pottage, Esau came in from the field, and he was famished. And Esau said to Jacob, "Let me eat some of that red pottage, for I am famished!" . . . Jacob said, "First sell me your birthright." Esau said, "I am about to die; of what use is a birthright to me?" Jacob said, "Swear to me first." So he swore to him, and sold his birthright to Jacob. Then Jacob gave

[1] Genesis 25:20–34; 27:1–6, 8–22, 24–29.

Esau bread and pottage of lentils, and he ate and drank, and rose and went his way. Thus Esau despised his birthright. . . .

When Isaac was old and his eyes were dim so that he could not see, he called Esau his older son, and said to him, "My son"; and he answered, "Here I am." He said, "Behold, I am old; I do not know the day of my death. Now then, take your weapons, your quiver and your bow, and go out to the field, and hunt game for me, and prepare for me savory food, such as I love, and bring it to me that I may eat; that I may bless you before I die."

Now Rebekah was listening when Isaac spoke to his son Esau. So when Esau went to the field to hunt for game and bring it, Rebekah said to her son Jacob, . . . "Now therefore, my son, . . . go to the flock, and fetch me two good kids, that I may prepare from them savory food for your father, such as he loves; and you shall bring it to your father to eat, so that he may bless you before he dies." But Jacob said to Rebekah his mother, "Behold, my brother Esau is a hairy man, and I am a smooth man. Perhaps my father will feel me, and I shall seem to be mocking him, and bring a curse upon myself and not a blessing." His mother said to him, "Upon me be your curse, my son; only obey my word, and go, fetch them to me." So he went and took them and brought them to his mother; and his mother prepared savory food, such as his father loved. Then Rebekah took the best garments of Esau her older son, which were with her in the house, and put them on Jacob her younger son; and the skins of the kids she put upon his hands and upon the smooth part of his neck; and she gave the savory food and the bread, which she had prepared, into the hand of her son Jacob.

So he went in to his father, and said, "My father"; and he said, "Here I am; who are you, my son?" Jacob said to his father, "I am Esau your first-born. I have done as you told me; now sit up and eat of my game, that you may bless me." But Isaac said to his son, "How is it that you have found it so quickly, my son?" He answered, "Because the LORD your God granted me success." Then Isaac said to Jacob, "Come near, that I may feel you, my son, to know whether you are really my son Esau or not." So Jacob went near to Isaac his father, who felt him and said, "The voice is Jacob's voice, but the hands are the hands of Esau." . . . He said, "Are you really my son Esau?" He answered, "I am." Then he said, "Bring it to me, that I may eat of my son's game and bless you." So he brought it to him, and he ate; and he brought him wine, and he drank. Then his father Isaac said to him, "Come near and kiss me, my son." So he came near and kissed him; and he smelled the smell of his garments, and blessed him, and said,

"See, the smell of my son
    is as the smell of a field which the LORD has blessed!
May God give you of the dew of heaven,
    and of the fatness of the earth,
    and plenty of grain and wine.
Let peoples serve you,
    and nations bow down to you.
Be lord over your brothers,
    and may your mother's sons bow down to you.
Cursed be every one who curses you,
    and blessed be every one who blesses you!"

Meditation 1: The First Coming of Christ

In the genealogy of Jesus offered by Matthew in the first chapter of his Gospel, he begins with "Abraham was the father of Isaac, and Isaac the father of Jacob" (Mt 1:2) and ends with "Joseph the husband of Mary, of whom Jesus was born, who is called Christ" (Mt 1:16). Isaac certainly did not start his life in a way that would set him up as an admirable patriarch of Israel and a noble kinsmen of the Messiah. But Isaac was by no means the most questionable of Jesus' lineage. To address just a few in Matthew's genealogy: Rahab was a prostitute and traitor, Manasseh was a pagan and mass murderer, and even the great King David was an adulterer and murderer.

Throughout salvation history, from the very story of creation, God promises his people that he will send the Messiah to save them, but he does not tell them when this will happen. He does not tell them exactly what to expect the Messiah to look like. Rather, God requires them to wait and to trust. He uses extremely unworthy instruments to accomplish his purposes to prepare his people for a very unlikely Messiah — a simple carpenter's son born in a manger, who was, in fact, God Incarnate.

Meditation 2: The Second Coming of Christ

God is just, and there will ultimately be an accounting for all of our actions here on earth. When our Lord comes at the end of (our) time, we will face all of our sins and failings. But our Lord will not only be just but also merciful.

This is a strange story to ponder. Why would God allow the patriarchal birthright and blessing of his Chosen People to pass from Isaac to a conniving "mama's boy" like Jacob, rather than the first-born Esau?

On the one hand, we might just have to accept that God does not judge as we judge because God sees far beyond what we see. This is a good spiritual practice because we will not always be able to see God's plan clearly. We often must act in trust that somehow, regardless of our comprehension, God's "will" will be done.

On the other hand, this story perhaps reveals the great wisdom of God. Implied in this story is the fact that Esau is a brash, arrogant, brutish man that cares little for his birthright and only cares about a blessing that will benefit him. As we read further the story of Jacob, we learn that he later is tried by God and undergoes purgation. He comes back to his family after proving his worth, reconciles with Esau, and carries on the patriarchal line of Abraham.

We must be ever mindful of the fact that God is coming. Regardless of what we have done in the past, we have the ability to make decisions now that will prepare us for Christ's future coming. Our past does not define us. Rather, our "today" does. Let us make the correct decision today that will bring us to the desired tomorrow. What past sin must you allow God to forgive? To what perceived failure are you grasping so tightly that you cannot receive the unfathomable gifts and glorious future God desires to give to you?

Meditation 3: The Third Coming of Christ

Jesus came from a broken family tree, just like us. His mother was likely suspected of being an adulteress. His ancestors were guilty of genocide, infanticide, witchcraft, polygamy, adultery, and prostitution. Jesus lived in anonymity for years. He worked for a living. He was not accepted by his close relatives, and he was hated by the leaders of his people. In fact, they put him to death.

Jesus understands our dirty, complicated lives. Jesus experienced all of the depravity of the human condition. He was intimately acquainted with sin in all of its forms. He comes to us personally despite our sins and failures. Is guilt or shame keeping you away from God? Do you believe that our Lord cannot love you exactly as you are? He does love us as we are, infinitely and intimately. The Gospel is full of references to Jesus healing and embracing the worst of sinners. Let our Lord Emmanuel, "God with us" (Mt 1:23), come into your life today in a new way. Invite him in. Say to Jesus, "Come, Lord. . . . Come to me just as I am. Come, Lord. Come!"

DECEMBER 8

Reading: Jacob — Renewal of the Covenant[1]

Then Isaac called Jacob and blessed him, and charged him, "You shall not marry one of the Canaanite women. Arise, go to Pad dan-ar am to the house of Bethu el your mother's father; and take as wife from there one of the daughters of La ban your mother's brother. God Almighty bless you and make you fruitful and multiply you, that you may become a company of peoples. May he give the blessing of Abraham to you and to your descendants with you, that you may take possession of the land of your sojournings which God gave to Abraham!" . . .

Jacob left Be er-she ba, and went toward Haran. And he came to a certain place, and stayed there that night, because the sun had set. Taking one of the stones of the place, he put it under his head and lay down in that place to sleep. And he dreamed that there was a ladder set up on the earth, and the top of it reached to heaven; and behold, the angels of God were ascending and descending on it! And behold, the LORD stood above it a and said, "I am the LORD, the God of Abraham your father and the God of Isaac; the land on which you lie I will give to you and to your descendants; and your descendants shall be like the dust of the earth, and you shall spread abroad to the west and to the east and to the north and to the south; and by you and your descendants shall all the families of the earth bless themselves. Behold, I am with you and will keep you wherever you go, and will bring you back to this land; for I will not leave you until I have done that of which I have spoken to you." . . .

[1] Genesis 28:1–4, 10–15; 29:1–2, 4–6, 12–13; 31:3, 17–18; 32:22–28.

Then Jacob went on his journey, and came to the land of the people of the east. As he looked, he saw a well in the field, and behold, three flocks of sheep lying beside it. . . .

Jacob said to [the shepherds], "My brothers, where do you come from?" They said, "We are from Haran." He said to them, "Do you know Laban the son of Nahor?" They said, "We know him." He said to them, "Is it well with him?" They said, "It is well; and see, Rachel his daughter is coming with the sheep!" . . .

Jacob told Rachel that he was her father's kinsman, and that he was Rebekah's son; and she ran and told her father.

When Laban heard the tidings of Jacob his sister's son, he ran to meet him, and embraced him and kissed him, and brought him to his house. . . [Jacob stayed with Laban and married both of Laban's daughters and their two maidservants in exchange for fourteen years of work for Laban. They bore him eleven sons: Reuben, Simeon, Levi, Judah, Dan, Naphtali, Gad, Asher, Issachar, Zebulun, and Joseph, and one daughter Dinah.]

Then the LORD said to Jacob, "Return to the land of your fathers and to your kindred, and I will be with you." . . . So Jacob arose, and set his sons and his wives on camels; and he drove away all his cattle, all his livestock which he had gained, the cattle in his possession which he had acquired in Paddan-aram, to go to the land of Canaan to his father Isaac. . . .

[Jacob] took his two wives, his two maids, and his eleven children, and crossed the ford of the Jabbok. He took them and sent them across the stream, and likewise everything that he had. And Jacob was left alone; and a man wrestled with him until the breaking of the day. When the man saw that he did not prevail against Jacob, he touched the hollow of his thigh; and Jacob's thigh was put out of joint as he wrestled with him. Then he said, "Let me go, for the day is breaking." But Jacob said, "I will not let you go, unless you bless me." And he said to him, "What is your name?"

And he said, "Jacob." Then he said, "Your name shall no more be called Jacob, but Israel, for you have striven with God and with men, and have prevailed."

Meditation 1: The First Coming of Christ

In this passage, we begin to see God fulfill his promise to the patriarchs that will culminate in the coming of the Messiah. God promised Adam, Noah, Abraham, and Isaac that they would be the fathers of a great nation with countless heirs. As the next patriarch in the line of descent, Jacob begins to taste the fruits of this promise. He is blessed with eleven boys and a girl (and will have another son, Benjamin, born to Rebekah in the land of Canaan). Jacob left his family with nothing and returned with wives, children, camels, and livestock.

Jacob sees a vision of angels ascending and descending a stairway that spanned between earth and Heaven. Jesus refers to this vision in his words to Nathanael — one whom Jesus refers to as "an Israelite indeed, in whom is no guile" (Jn 1:47) — "I say to you, you will see heaven opened, and the angels of God ascending and descending upon the Son of Man" (Jn 1:51). In this, Jesus recalls the vision of Israel (Jacob), who was duplicitous while speaking to a true Israelite without duplicity (Nathanael). Jacob saw a vision of a ladder that would unite Heaven and earth. Jesus reveals to Nathanael that, as the Messiah, he is the ladder that will unite Heaven and earth.

It is valuable to compare Jacob to Jesus. Jacob did not have the best start. He connived to get his brother's birthright and his father's blessing. He toiled many years under the oppression of Laban to obtain his rightful inheritance and dowry. He "wrestled with God" figuratively (and literally) until he was ready to enter into the land of his father and take up the role of patriarch. Like

Abraham, when he aligned himself to God's will, Jacob was given a new name by God, signifying his new role.

Conversely, Jesus was always obedient to the will of the Father. He wrestled only with the devil but was a sign of contradiction and struggle for many who could not accept that he was the Messiah. Jesus bore many names, each signifying a unique role (e.g., Christ/Messiah, Son of God, Son of Man, and Word made flesh).

Meditation 2: The Second Coming of Christ

The story of Jacob's life drives home the words of St. Paul, "For here we have no lasting city, but we seek the city which is to come" (Heb 13:14). Jacob was a wanderer, looking for peace and blessing. He had to flee his homeland for fear of his brother's vengeance. Through great hardship and toil, Jacob obtained a large family and many possessions. (Consider reading the omitted verses of this account [Genesis, chapters 29 and 30] to get a full understanding of the trials that Laban put Jacob through.) Even then, he could not settle down and enjoy the fruits of his efforts. Rather, he needed to return to the land of his father. There he had to dissuade his brother from seeking vengeance. Even after that, Jacob found no rest in the land but, ultimately, had to move his entire clan to Egypt to flee famine (we will read about this in the upcoming days).

We, like Jacob, are the nomads to whom St. Paul is referring. There is no lasting peace here on earth. Regardless of our toils, we will experience grief and suffering. Ultimately, we will die and meet our Lord face to face. This is not our lasting city, and our Lord coming to us in death is not something to be feared. It is the source of our hope. It is the eternal city of Heaven for which our hearts long.

St. Augustine remarked that our hearts are restless and will remain restless until they rest in God. We were made by God, for God. It is in God that we find our true meaning and joy. It is in God that we find our purpose and completion. And it is in God that we find true joy and peace.

We cannot fathom the splendor of Heaven. For "no eye has seen, nor ear heard, nor the heart of man conceived, what God has prepared for those who love him" (1 Co 2:9). Let us not then get caught up in the trials and tribulations of this world or even distracted by its beauties and allurements. Rather, let us keep our eyes on our true and perfect destination. What are you placing into the hole in your heart that only God can fill?

Meditation 3: The Third Coming of Christ

As God sends Jacob forth from his home, he assures Jacob, "I am with you and will keep you wherever you go" (Gn 28:15). When God tells Jacob to return, he assures Jacob, "I will be with you" (Gn 31:3). The last words of Jesus to his Apostles are these same words, "I am with you always" (Mt 28:20).

Our Lord is with us in every moment of our existence. He sustains our lives and all life around us. We have received the very divine life of God at our Baptism. And he dwells within our souls.

Our Lord is truly present — Body, Blood, Soul, and Divinity — in the Eucharist. He is present in every Tabernacle in the world. He enters into us in an unfathomable way every time we receive him in Holy Communion.

Our Lord watches over us every moment of every day. He listens to us when we speak to him. God is never distracted. We always have his undivided attention. And God constantly speaks to us — through Scripture, through the words of the priest at Mass and in Confession, through the good counsel of others around us, and directly to our hearts, if we will listen.

God is with us. He loves us. He listens to us. And he speaks to us. Will you acknowledge his presence? Will you receive his love? Will you cry out to him? Will you listen to him?

DECEMBER 9

Reading: Joseph — Dream and Betrayal[1]

Now Israel loved Joseph more than any other of his children, because he was the son of his old age; and he made him a long robe with sleeves. But when his brothers saw that their father loved him more than all his brothers, they hated him, and could not speak peaceably to him.

Now Joseph had a dream, and when he told it to his brothers they only hated him the more. He said to them, "Hear this dream which I have dreamed: behold, we were binding sheaves in the field, and behold, my sheaf arose and stood upright; and behold, your sheaves gathered round it, and bowed down to my sheaf." His brothers said to him, "Are you indeed to reign over us? Or are you indeed to have dominion over us?" So they hated him yet more for his dreams and for his words. Then he dreamed another dream, and told it to his brothers, and said, "Behold, I have dreamed another dream; and behold, the sun, the moon, and eleven stars were bowing down to me." But when he told it to his father and to his brothers, his father rebuked him, and said to him, "What is this dream that you have dreamed? Shall I and your mother and your brothers indeed come to bow ourselves to the ground before you?" And his brothers were jealous of him, but his father kept the saying in mind.

Now his brothers went to pasture their father's flock near She'chem. And Israel said to Joseph, "Are not your brothers pasturing the flock at She'chem? Come, I will send you to them." . . .

---

[1] Genesis 37:3–13, 18–28, 31–36.

They saw him afar off, and before he came near to them they conspired against him to kill him. They said to one another, "Here comes this dreamer. Come now, let us kill him and throw him into one of the pits; then we shall say that a wild beast has devoured him, and we shall see what will become of his dreams." But when Reuben heard it, he delivered him out of their hands, saying, "Let us not take his life." And Reuben said to them, "Shed no blood; cast him into this pit here in the wilderness, but lay no hand upon him" — that he might rescue him out of their hand, to restore him to his father. So when Joseph came to his brothers, they stripped him of his robe, the long robe with sleeves that he wore; and they took him and cast him into a pit. . . .

They saw a caravan of Ish'maelites coming from Gilead, with their camels bearing gum, balm, and myrrh, on their way to carry it down to Egypt. Then Judah said to his brothers, "What profit is it if we slay our brother and conceal his blood? Come, let us sell him to the Ish'maelites, and let not our hand be upon him, for he is our brother, our own flesh." And his brothers heeded him. Then Mid'ianite traders passed by; and they drew Joseph up and lifted him out of the pit, and sold him to the Ish'maelites for twenty shekels of silver; and they took Joseph to Egypt. . . .

Then they took Joseph's robe, and killed a goat, and dipped the robe in the blood; and they sent the long robe with sleeves and brought it to their father, and said, "This we have found; see now whether it is your son's robe or not." And he recognized it, and said, "It is my son's robe; a wild beast has devoured him; Joseph is without doubt torn to pieces." Then Jacob tore his garments, and put sackcloth upon his loins, and mourned for his son many days. All his sons and all his daughters rose up to comfort him; but he refused to be comforted, and said, "No, I shall go down to Sheol to my son, mourning." Thus his father wept for him. Meanwhile the Mid'ianites had sold him in Egypt to Pot'iphar, an officer of Pharaoh, the captain of the guard.

Meditation 1: The First Coming of Christ

Like Isaac, Joseph is an Old Testament prefigurement (or "type") of Christ. Joseph, like Jesus, suffers unjustly at the hands of his "brothers." In sharing his dream, Joseph should not be seen to have been bragging to his father and brothers. He was merely stating a truth — not only that he had this dream but also (as we will learn later) a dream that would come true. Joseph's brothers did not want to hear the truth because of their jealousy. Similarly, the relatives and townspeople of Nazareth were offended when Jesus read Isaiah's messianic prophecy in the synagogue and then said, in effect, "I am the Messiah prophesied by Isaiah" (see Lk 4:16–30). Joseph's brothers sought to kill him by throwing him into a pit. The townspeople sought to kill Jesus by throwing him off a hill. Neither murder attempt was successful, and God's plan continued to unfold.

Joseph was taunted, stripped, abused, and given over to the pagan Egyptians. Jesus was taunted, stripped, abused, and given over to the pagan Romans. Both Joseph's slavery and Christ's death seemed to be the end of the story. But, in both cases, it was only the beginning. Joseph (as we will learn in the next days' readings) became the means of deliverance of his family from starvation (physical death). Jesus rose from the dead and became the source of deliverance of all mankind from sin and (eternal) death.

Today, we would benefit from meditating on the suffering of Christ and the victory it won in the words of the Prophet Isaiah's "Song of the Suffering Servant" (Is 53:3, 5, 7, 10–12):

> He was despised and rejected by men;
>> a man of sorrows, and acquainted with grief. . . .
>
> He was wounded for our transgressions,
>> he was bruised for our iniquities. . . .
>
> He was oppressed, and he was afflicted,
>> yet he opened not his mouth;

like a lamb that is led to the slaughter,

    and like a sheep that before its shearers is silent. . . .

The will of the LORD shall prosper in his hand;

    he shall see the fruit of the travail of his soul and
    be satisfied. . . .

Therefore I will divide him a portion with the great,

    and he shall divide the spoil with the strong;

because he poured out his soul to death,

    and was numbered with the transgressors;

yet he bore the sin of many,

    and made intercession for the transgressors.

Meditation 2: The Second Coming of Christ

There are many sufferings that come our way here on earth, which inspire the age-old question, "Why would a loving God allow suffering?" This story of Joseph provides an answer.

First, God allows us to suffer because he loves us and has given us the ability to love him in return. Love requires free will. For God to love us, he must not dominate us, and so he creates us with the gift of freedom. For us to be able to love God in return, we must have the freedom to love him in return or reject him. Free will allows for both good and bad decisions. Bad decisions have bad consequences. God loved Joseph and his father, Israel, but he also loved Joseph's brothers. In that love, God allowed Joseph's brothers to freely choose evil and subject Joseph and his father to great suffering.

Second, the evil of this world and the consequences thereof are not the end. Our suffering here on earth will end; the glory of Heaven will be eternal. Hope is the antidote for suffering. We hope in the Resurrection and eternal joy of Heaven when every tear will be wiped away. In the midst of our suffering here on earth, we look to our destiny and cry out with St. Paul, "I consider that the sufferings of this present time are not worth comparing with the glory that is to be revealed to us" (Rm 8:18).

Third, God's plan is never thwarted by our evil acts. All of our disobedient acts and resultant suffering can be occasions for God to reveal his love and glory. As we will learn in the upcoming days' readings, this betrayal of Joseph did not end in suffering but in great joy and good for the entire family of Israel.

While we are headed toward Heaven, we currently live in a broken world full of suffering. What suffering have you experienced that has not healed? Is there someone whom you have not forgiven? Are you struggling to forgive yourself? Let God help you forgive. Let God help you heal. Hope in God's mercy because the eternal joy of Heaven begins today.

Meditation 3: The Third Coming of Christ

God speaks to us daily in various and unsuspected ways. God spoke to Joseph in dreams to prepare him for an extraordinary future in which he, the second youngest of the house of Israel, would surpass all of his brothers and lead the people chosen by God into a time of great growth and prosperity, resulting in the nation that would ultimately be led into the Promised Land by Moses. God was also speaking to Israel and Joseph's brothers in these dreams, assuring them that Joseph would deliver them from their future time of peril. Their pride prevented them, however, from hearing God's message, and they rebelled against it.

When the brothers of Joseph would not listen to his original message, God spoke to them in another way. God touched the heart of Reuben, inspiring him to show mercy. Reuben was the eldest, who would, by his birthright, be expected to be the heir of Israel and the next patriarch. As such, Reuben had the most reason to be insulted by Israel's favoritism shown to Joseph and Joseph's dream suggesting his superiority. Yet Reuben begged his brothers not to murder Joseph and even planned to return Joseph to his father's protection. Despite the malice in their hearts, the brothers heard, at least faintly, God's appeal in the words of Reuben. They spared the life of Joseph and instead sold him into slavery.

Our Lord approaches us daily and speaks to us in so many ways. Why do we not hear the message? Is it that we do not truly believe that God is concerned for us, or do we simply not listen? Does our pride get in the way — do we have a preconceived notion of what God should say to us and how he should speak to us? Does our selfishness prevent us from hearing God — do we place our own desires above those of the God who loved us so much that he created us from nothing, suffered, died, and rose for us?

DECEMBER 10

Reading: Joseph in Egypt[1]

Now Joseph was taken down to Egypt, and Pot íphar, an officer of Pharaoh, the captain of the guard, an Egyptian, bought him from the Ish ́maelites who had brought him down there. The LORD was with Joseph, and he became a successful man, . . . and his master saw that the LORD was with him, and that the LORD caused all that he did to prosper in his hands. So Joseph found favor in his sight and attended him, and he made him overseer of his house and put him in charge of all that he had. . . .

Now Joseph was handsome and good-looking. And after a time his master's wife cast her eyes upon Joseph, and said, "Lie with me." But he refused. . . . But one day, when he went into the house to do his work and none of the men of the house was there in the house, she caught him by his garment, saying, "Lie with me." But he left his garment in her hand, and fled and got out of the house. . . . Then she laid up his garment by her until his master came home, and she told him, . . . "The Hebrew servant, whom you have brought among us, came in to me to insult me; but as soon as I lifted up my voice and cried, he left his garment with me, and fled out of the house."

When his master heard the words which his wife spoke to him . . . his anger was kindled. And Joseph's master took him and put him into the prison. . . . But the LORD was with Joseph and showed him mercy, and gave him favor in the sight of the keeper of the prison.

[1] Genesis 39:1–4, 6–8, 11–12, 16–22; 41:1–8, 14, 25–27, 29–30, 33–36, 39–40, 46–48, 53–54, 57.

And the keeper of the prison committed to Joseph's care all the prisoners who were in the prison. . . .

After two whole years, Pharaoh dreamed that he was standing by the Nile, and behold there came up out of the Nile seven cows sleek and fat, and they fed in the reed grass. And behold, seven other cows, gaunt and thin, came up out of the Nile after them, and stood by the other cows on the bank of the Nile. And the gaunt and thin cows ate up the seven sleek and fat cows. And Pharaoh awoke. And he fell asleep and dreamed a second time; and behold, seven ears of grain, plump and good, were growing on one stalk. And behold, after them sprouted seven ears, thin and blighted by the east wind. And the thin ears swallowed up the seven plump and full ears. . . . So in the morning his spirit was troubled; and he sent and called for all the magicians of Egypt and all its wise men; and Pharaoh told them his dream, but there was none who could interpret it to Pharaoh. . . .

Then Pharaoh sent and called Joseph [because his steward, while previously in prison, had a dream interpreted correctly by Joseph], and they brought him hastily out of the dungeon [and Pharaoh told Joseph his dream]. . . .

Then Joseph said to Pharaoh, ". . . God has revealed to Pharaoh what he is about to do. The seven good cows are seven years, and the seven good ears are seven years. . . . The seven lean and gaunt cows that came up after them are seven years, and the seven empty ears blighted by the east wind are also seven years of famine. . . . There will come seven years of great plenty throughout all the land of Egypt, but after them there will arise seven years of famine, and all the plenty will be forgotten in the land of Egypt. . . . Now therefore let Pharaoh select a man discreet and wise, and set him over the land of Egypt. Let Pharaoh proceed to appoint overseers over the land, and take the fifth part of the produce of the land of Egypt during the seven plenteous years. And let them gather all the food of these good years that are coming, and lay up grain under the authority of Pharaoh for food in the cities, and let them keep it. That food shall be a reserve for the land against the seven years of famine which are to befall the land of Egypt, so that the land may not perish through the famine." . . .

So Pharaoh said to Joseph, "Since God has shown you all this, there is none so discreet and wise as you are; you shall be over my house, and all my people shall order themselves as you command." . . .

Joseph went out from the presence of Pharaoh, and went through all the land of Egypt. During the seven plenteous years the earth brought forth abundantly, and he gathered up all the food of the seven years when there was plenty in the land of Egypt, and stored up food in the cities. . . .

The seven years of plenty that prevailed in the land of Egypt came to an end; and the seven years of famine began to come, as Joseph had said. There was famine in all lands; but in all the land of Egypt there was bread. . . . All the earth came to Egypt to Joseph to buy grain, because the famine was severe over all the earth.

Meditation 1: The First Coming of Christ

Like Jesus, Joseph was an innocent man, mistreated by his kin and subject to great hardship. Joseph's imprisonment is symbolic of Jesus' death. A "nobody" Hebrew slave would have no expectation of release and would undoubtedly die in prison. Isaiah's words might equally speak to both Joseph and Jesus (Is 53:8–12):

He was cut off from the land of the living. . . .

And they made his grave with the wicked . . .

although he had done no violence,

and there was no deceit in his mouth.

Yet it was the will of the LORD to bruise him; . . .

> he shall see his offspring, he shall prolong his days;
> the will of the LORD shall prosper in his hand;
>> he shall see the fruit of the travail of his soul and be satisfied. . . .
> Therefore I will divide him a portion with the great,
>> and he shall divide the spoil with the strong.

Just as prison was not to be the end of Joseph, death was not to be Jesus' finality. Joseph came out from prison and was elevated to the right hand of Pharaoh. Jesus came out from the tomb and took his place at the right hand of the Father. Joseph was set in command over all Egypt, and all the peoples from throughout the land came and prostrated themselves before him. Jesus took his rightful place as Lord of all.

Joseph became an instrument for feeding God's people. He provided the bread they needed to live through the time of physical famine. Similarly, Jesus feeds God's people with the Eucharist — the "Bread of Life" we need to live through the spiritual famine caused by sin. The bread provided by Joseph sustained the people for a few years. The Body, Blood, Soul, and Divinity of Christ's Real Presence in the Eucharist feeds us for eternity.

Meditation 2: The Second Coming of Christ

Potiphar's wife sought to have Joseph enter into an illicit relationship with her. Joseph could have given in to this pleasure. Assuming she wished to be discreet, Joseph would have avoided imprisonment by consenting. Joseph refused. He did what was right. And the immediate consequence was imprisonment.

Fortunately for Joseph, his imprisonment did not end in physical death. Because of his ability to interpret the dream of a fellow prisoner, Joseph was called to assist Pharaoh, who rewarded him with power and prestige. But Joseph could not foresee this consequence. He merely did what was right, not counting the cost, and trusted that God would see things to a good end.

Our choices have many consequences. Some are immediate. And some are delayed. But we must always be mindful of the ultimate consequences of our actions, despite the more proximate, especially when it comes to eternal consequences. We can make many choices to lie, cheat, and act in ways that bring about immediate gratification. Or we can make tough choices that will result in some amount of pain and suffering here on earth but are right and good.

We must be mindful that we will be called to stand before the throne of God and answer for our actions. God will separate the sheep (those who accepted God's way and sacrificed for others) from the goats (those who ignored God and lived for their own well-being alone). All the pleasures of this world pale in comparison to the eternal love, joy, and peace of the Second Coming of Christ. What tough choice stands before you? Will you ask God to give you the strength to do the right thing?

Meditation 3: The Third Coming of Christ

Our Lord comes into our lives every day in mysterious and unexpected ways. His will for us is often hidden but always ordered toward our ultimate good.

Joseph would naturally believe that his betrayal by his brothers and slavery would lead to a short, unhappy, and inglorious life. The opposite was true. They were means to the salvation of his family.

Our Lord was with Joseph in his service of Potiphar, causing "all that he did to prosper in his hands" (Gn 39:3). Our Lord was with Joseph in the depth of prison, giving him "favor in the sight of the keeper of the prison" (Gn 39:21), who entrusted into Joseph's care all of the prisoners. Our Lord revealed the meaning of a fellow prisoner's dream, leading to Joseph's opportunity to interpret Pharaoh's dream.

At so many points in Joseph's life, he could have despaired and doubted God's concern for him. Yet he remained faithful and saw God's corresponding faithfulness and care for him. Where are the dark places in our lives when we doubt God's love or even his existence? Our Lord is still there in these places, in these moments. We may not see him. We may not feel him. But he is there. These are the moments when we must cry out, "Jesus I trust in you!"

DECEMBER 11

Reading: Joseph — Reunion; The Tribes of Israel Move to Egypt[1]

When Jacob learned that there was grain in Egypt, he said to his sons, "Why do you look at one another?" And he said, "Behold, I have heard that there is grain in Egypt; go down and buy grain for us there, that we may live, and not die." . . .

Now Joseph was governor over the land; he it was who sold to all the people of the land. And Joseph's brothers came, and bowed themselves before him with their faces to the ground. . . . Thus Joseph knew his brothers, but they did not know him. And Joseph remembered the dreams which he had dreamed of them. . . .

And Joseph said to his brothers, "I am Joseph; is my father still alive?" . . .

Joseph said to his brothers, "Come near to me, I beg you." And they came near. And he said, "I am your brother, Joseph, whom you sold into Egypt. And now do not be distressed, or angry with yourselves, because you sold me here; for God sent me before you to preserve life. For the famine has been in the land these two years; and there are yet five years in which there will be neither plowing nor harvest. And God sent me before you to preserve for you a remnant on earth, and to keep alive for you many survivors. So it was not you who sent me here, but God; and he has made me a father to Pharaoh, and lord of all his house and ruler over all the land of Egypt. Make haste and go up to my father and say to him, 'Thus says your son Joseph, God has made

[1] Genesis 42:1–2, 6, 8–9; 45:3–10, 25–28; 46:5–7, 29–30.

me lord of all Egypt; come down to me, do not tarry; you shall dwell in the land of Go shen, and you shall be near me, you and your children and your children's children, and your flocks, your herds, and all that you have. . . .

So they went up out of Egypt, and came to the land of Canaan to their father Jacob. And they told him, "Joseph is still alive, and he is ruler over all the land of Egypt." And his heart fainted, for he did not believe them. But when they told him all the words of Joseph, which he had said to them, and when he saw the wagons which Joseph had sent to carry him, the spirit of their father Jacob revived; and Israel said, "It is enough; Joseph my son is still alive; I will go and see him before I die." . . .

Then Jacob set out from Be 'er-she ba; and the sons of Israel carried Jacob their father, their little ones, and their wives, in the wagons which Pharaoh had sent to carry him. They also took their cattle and their goods, which they had gained in the land of Canaan, and came into Egypt, Jacob and all his offspring with him, his sons, and his sons' sons with him, his daughters, and his sons' daughters; all his offspring he brought with him into Egypt. . . .

Then Joseph made ready his chariot and went up to meet Israel his father in Go shen; and he presented himself to him, and fell on his neck, and wept on his neck a good while. Israel said to Joseph, "Now let me die, since I have seen your face and know that you are still alive."

Meditation 1: The First Coming of Christ

In Joseph, we see a foreshadowing of how Jesus would accomplish salvation in his role as the "suffering servant." Isaiah proclaims, "He was wounded for our transgressions, he was bruised for our iniquities; upon him was the chastisement that made us whole, and with his stripes we are healed" (Is 53:5).

For both Joseph and Jesus, their condemnation and abuse by God's people was the instrument by which their salvation was obtained. Joseph was condemned by his brothers and handed over to the Ishmaelites. This led to his elevation as overseer of all Egypt. In this role, Joseph saved God's people from famine and welcomed them into a land of wealth and provision. Jesus was condemned by his people and handed over to the Romans. This led to his Crucifixion, death, and Resurrection. By this, Jesus took upon himself the sin of all and welcomed all people into Heaven.

God allowed these innocents, Joseph and Jesus, to bear the iniquity of the sinful. They were made to suffer by and for those who deserved to suffer. The very suffering caused by God's sinful people was the means by which those who caused the suffering were saved.

Meditation 2: The Second Coming of Christ

Two themes of this reading are particularly useful in meditating upon the Second Coming of Christ. The first is the fact that we should not take Heaven for granted. The second is that of recognition.

Joseph tells his brothers that God made him the lord of all Egypt and tasked him to preserve a remnant and to keep alive many survivors (see Gn 45:7). This saving of some, but not all, is consistent with other stories we have encountered thus far in our Advent readings (e.g., the call of Abraham and some but not all of his clan, and the saving of Noah and his family but the destruction of the rest of the people of earth).

In the end, Jesus, the Lord of all creation, will come again and complete his salvific activity. All will stand before the throne and be judged. Not all will enter the Kingdom of Heaven. Even a cursory reading of Scripture confirms this truth — the separation of the wheat from the chaff (see Mt 3:12); the separation of the sheep from the goats (see Mt 25:31–46); "Not every one who says to me, 'Lord, Lord,' shall enter the kingdom of heaven" (Mt 7:21–23); "Many are called, but few are chosen" (Mt 22:14); and "For the gate is wide and the way easy, that leads to destruction, and those who enter it are many. For the gate is narrow and the way is hard, that leads to life, and those who enter it are few" (Mt 7:13–14). The sobering reality of Hell should not cause us to despair. Rather, it should motivate us to desire Heaven.

The theme of recognition is particularly poignant. Like Joseph, Jesus knows us and wants us to recognize him, especially in those we encounter every day. When we stand before the throne, we do not want to hear the words, "I never knew you; depart from me, you evildoers" (Mt 7:23). Rather, let us always seek to recognize Jesus in the face of those afflicted by hunger, thirst, sickness, imprisonment, and other needs and strive to meet those needs. Then, we need not live in fear of Hell but may look forward to hearing the words of our Lord: "Come, O blessed of my Father, inherit the kingdom prepared for you from the foundation of the world" (Mt 25:34). If you were to stand before the Lord today, would you recognize him? Would he recognize you?

Meditation 3: The Third Coming of Christ

Joseph's brothers came face to face with Joseph but did not know him. Joseph knew them, but they did not know him. So Joseph revealed himself and forgave them with the words, "Do not be distressed, or angry with yourselves, because you sold me" (Gn 45:5), and lavished good things upon them.

After his Resurrection, Jesus appeared to Mary Magdalene, but she did not recognize him (see Jn 20:11–18). Jesus approached two of his disciples on the road to Emmaus, but they did not recognize him (see Lk 24:13–35). Jesus called out to a group of the

Apostles fishing, but they did not recognize him (see Jn 21:1–14). Jesus then revealed himself to them, forgave them for their abandonment of him, and invited them into a new life born of the reality of his Resurrection. Not only did Jesus forgive Peter for his denial and abandonment, but he gave him the entire Church to shepherd (see Jn 21:15–19)

Jesus knows each of us intimately. He knows exactly who we are, including all of our failings. He reveals himself. He offers complete forgiveness of our sins. Like Joseph, he begs us not to be distressed over our betrayal of him. He invites us every day to follow him. He offers eternal life with him. We can never earn God's love. We do not have to. It is constantly offered by God to us, and we must merely accept it in gratitude. Will you allow God to forgive you for past failings and accept his mercy?

DECEMBER 12

Reading: Moses and the Burning Bush[1]

Then Joseph died, and all his brothers, and all that generation. But the descendants of Israel were fruitful and increased greatly; they multiplied and grew exceedingly strong; so that the land was filled with them. . . .

Then Pharaoh commanded all his people, "Every son that is born to the Hebrews you shall cast into the Nile, but you shall let every daughter live."

Now a man from the house of Levi went and took to wife a daughter of Levi. The woman conceived and bore a son . . . and she hid him three months. And when she could hide him no longer she took for him a basket . . . and placed it among the reeds at the river's brink. . . . Now the daughter of Pharaoh came down to bathe at the river, and . . . she saw the basket among the reeds. . . . When she opened it she saw the child. . . . She took pity on him, . . . and he became her son; and she named him Moses, for she said, "Because I drew him out of the water."

One day, when Moses had grown up, he went out to his people and looked on their burdens; and he saw an Egyptian beating a Hebrew, one of his people. He looked this way and that, and seeing no one he killed the Egyptian and hid him in the sand. When he went out the next day, behold, two Hebrews were struggling together; and he said to the man that did the wrong, "Why do you strike your fellow?" He answered, "Who made you a prince and a judge over us? Do you mean to kill me as you killed the Egyptian?"

[1] Exodus 1:6–7, 22; 2:1–3, 5–6, 10–15, 3:1–2, 4, 6–8, 10–15, 19–20.

Then Moses was afraid, and thought, "Surely the thing is known." When Pharaoh heard of it, he sought to kill Moses.

But Moses fled from Pharaoh, and stayed in the land of Midian. . . .

Now Moses [having married] was keeping the flock of his father-in-law, Jethro, . . . and he led his flock . . . and came to Horeb, the mountain of God. And the angel of the LORD appeared to him in a flame of fire out of the midst of a bush; and he looked, and behold, the bush was burning, yet it was not consumed. . . . God called to him out of the bush, "Moses, Moses!" And he said, "Here am I." . . . And he said, "I am the God of your father, the God of Abraham, the God of Isaac, and the God of Jacob." And Moses hid his face, for he was afraid to look at God.

Then the LORD said, "I have seen the affliction of my people who are in Egypt, and have heard their cry because of their taskmasters; I know their sufferings, and I have come down to deliver them out of the hand of the Egyptians, and to bring them up out of that land to a good and broad land, a land flowing with milk and honey. . . . Come, I will send you to Pharaoh that you may bring forth my people, the sons of Israel, out of Egypt." But Moses said to God, "Who am I that I should go to Pharaoh, and bring the sons of Israel out of Egypt?" He said, "But I will be with you." . . .

Then Moses said to God, "If I come to the sons of Israel and say to them, 'The God of your fathers has sent me to you,' and they ask me, 'What is his name?' what shall I say to them?" God said to Moses, "I AM WHO I AM." And he said, "Say this to the sons of Israel, 'I AM has sent me to you.'" God also said to Moses, "Say this to the sons of Israel, 'The LORD, the God of your fathers, the God of Abraham, the God of Isaac, and the God of Jacob, has sent me to you': this is my name for ever, and thus I am to be remembered throughout all generations. . . . I know that the king of Egypt will not let you go unless compelled by a mighty hand.

So I will stretch out my hand and strike Egypt with all the wonders which I will do in it; after that he will let you go."

Meditation 1: The First Coming of Christ

Moses was sent by God as a prefigurement (or 'type") of Christ to prepare God's people for Christ's coming. Moses was hidden for three months; Christ would be hidden (in death) for three days. Moses, sentenced to death by Pharaoh before his birth, came through the waters of the Nile River to new life. Christ would enter into the waters of the Jordan River to be baptized by John so as to impart divine life to the waters of Christian Baptism and free all people from the death of Original Sin. Moses was saved through water and brought the people out of the death of slavery in Egypt to new life in the Promised Land. Because of Christ's institution of the Sacrament of Baptism, we, who are under a sentence of death through sin, come through the waters to new eternal life in Christ.

Moses had a dual identity. He was the natural child of God's Chosen People Israel and the adopted son of royalty. Likewise, Jesus possesses two natures. Jesus is both fully man and fully God. Eternally begotten, he is the Son of the Father. Born of Mary, he is a true son of Israel.

Moses prepared the people for the coming of Christ by bringing them into a much closer relationship with God. God revealed his name to the people through Moses. He confirmed the continuity of his relationship with them — that it was he who was the God of Abraham, Isaac, Jacob, and the people in Egyptian bondage. Through Moses, God called his people out from Egypt to be set apart from all others and to enter into the Promised Land. He moved them forward on a journey that would not end with their entry into a physical place here on earth but into a new spiritual home opened up by Christ.

Meditation 2: The Second Coming of Christ

How will we respond when God calls our name at the end of our lives? When God called out to Moses from the burning bush, "Moses hid his face, for he was afraid to look at God" (Ex 3:6). Maybe he hid his face out of reverence. Maybe he was trying to hide himself because of a real fear of God — who was this "God," and what would he do to Moses? There is certainly the possibility that Moses was afraid of God because Moses was a "murderer" (having killed the Egyptian), and, perhaps, he feared reprisal from God.

There is a theme in the Old Testament that one would die if one looked at God. One way to understand this fear is that the light of God would reveal all of one's sin and unworthiness, and God's glory would obliterate the person. Another explanation is that if God were to fully reveal himself to someone, the person would be so enamored with God's beauty that this earthly life would offer no attraction, and he would give up his life instantly to be with God. Both of these are useful in our meditation on the Second Coming of Christ.

Let us do all we can to make sure that when we come face to face with our Lord at the end of our lives, there are no unconfessed sins that would prevent us from entering into Heaven. Let us not fear God's coming but prepare for it daily. Let us seek every day to see more clearly God's beauty reflected in creation and, especially, in our neighbor. Let us strive to know God as intimately as we can so that, when we hear his call, we, unlike Moses, will know exactly who is calling us.

Meditation 3: The Third Coming of Christ

It is easy to fall into a belief that God comes into our lives powerfully only on very momentous occasions — when we are deep in prayer or calling out to God from the depths of our hearts. But this is simply not true. God comes to us at every moment, exactly where we are. He often chooses the most unexpected times to reach out to us most intimately. He also may ask of us the least likely thing we would expect.

Moses had escaped from Egypt, had gotten married, and was settling down into an unremarkable life. He was in the middle of a "normal workday," tending the sheep, when God approached him and turned his life upside down. God came to Moses and asked him to lead his people out from the grips of the most powerful nation on earth. It was especially surprising to Moses that he would be asked to be God's spokesman, as Moses had difficulty speaking (see Ex 4:10; 6:30).

God is never disengaged from us. He is never distracted. At every moment of our existence, God is completely and lovingly focused on each of us personally. There is no divided attention in God. From our perspective, it is as if we were the only person in creation. God never stops reaching out to us. We often find it hard to hear God speaking to us, but we seldom truly listen. Even what may appear to be silence may actually be God shouting out to us.

We must seek to put aside all fear of that which God asks of us. God does not always call the equipped but will always equip those whom he calls. If God wills us to accomplish something, he will accomplish it if we merely surrender our will and cooperate with him. It does not matter whether God speaks to us in a trumpet or a whisper. It does not matter whether he calls us to battle or humble surrender. Our perfection lies merely in a simple response to God's call: "Yes, Lord, thy will be done." Are you open to hearing God speak to you?

DECEMBER 13

Reading: The Exodus[1]

The LORD said to Moses, "Yet one plague more I will bring upon Pharaoh and upon Egypt; afterwards he will let you go from here. . . .

Then Moses called all the elders of Israel, and said to them, "Select lambs for yourselves according to your families, and kill the Passover lamb. Take a bunch of hyssop and dip it in the blood which is in the basin, and touch the lintel and the two doorposts with the blood which is in the basin; and none of you shall go out of the door of his house until the morning. For the LORD will pass through to slay the Egyptians; and when he sees the blood on the lintel and on the two doorposts, the LORD will pass over the door, and will not allow the destroyer to enter your houses to slay you. . . .

At midnight the LORD struck all the first-born in the land of Egypt, from the first-born of Pharaoh who sat on his throne to the first-born of the captive who was in the dungeon, and all the first-born of the cattle. And Pharaoh rose up in the night, he, and all his servants, and all the Egyptians; and there was a great cry in Egypt, for there was not a house where one was not dead. And he summoned Moses and Aaron by night, and said, "Rise up, go forth from among my people, both you and the sons of Israel; and go, serve the LORD, as you have said. Take your flocks and your herds, as you have said, and be gone; and bless me also!" . . .

When the king of Egypt was told that the people had fled, the mind of Pharaoh and his servants was changed toward the people,

[1]   Exodus 11:1; 12:21–23, 29–32; 14:5–6, 8, 10–11, 13, 21–23, 26–27, 30–31.

and they said, "What is this we have done, that we have let Israel go from serving us?" So he made ready his chariot and took his army with him, . . . and he pursued the sons of Israel. . . .

When Pharaoh drew near, the sons of Israel lifted up their eyes, and behold, the Egyptians were marching after them; and they were in great fear. And the sons of Israel cried out to the LORD; and they said to Moses, "Is it because there are no graves in Egypt that you have taken us away to die in the wilderness?" . . . And Moses said to the people, "Fear not, stand firm, and see the salvation of the LORD, which he will work for you today."

Then Moses stretched out his hand over the sea; and the LORD drove the sea back by a strong east wind all night, and made the sea dry land, and the waters were divided. And the sons of Israel went into the midst of the sea on dry ground, the waters being a wall to them on their right hand and on their left. The Egyptians pursued, and went in after them into the midst of the sea. . . .

Then the LORD said to Moses, "Stretch out your hand over the sea, that the water may come back upon the Egyptians." . . . So Moses stretched forth his hand over the sea, and the sea returned to its usual flow, . . . and the LORD routed the Egyptians in the midst of the sea. . . .

Thus the LORD saved Israel that day from the hand of the Egyptians. . . . And Israel saw the great work which the LORD did against the Egyptians, and the people feared the LORD; and they believed in the LORD and in his servant Moses.

Meditation 1: The First Coming of Christ

The Passover lamb of the Exodus foreshadows Jesus, who is the true and eternal Passover Lamb. The Israelites ate the lamb as a family and spread its blood on their doors. Thus, they were saved from death. The lamb was food for the journey they were about to embark upon, from Egypt, across the desert, to the Promised Land.

In instituting the Eucharist at the Last Supper, Jesus, the Lamb of God, gave us his flesh to eat. While Jesus' flesh is "true food" (Jn 6:55), it is not mere physical sustenance but "super-essential" bread that nourishes the body and soul. In consuming the Eucharist, we receive the very Body, Blood, Soul, and Divinity of Jesus. It is food for the journey of life. It sustains us with the grace to help us travel from slavery to sin, across the desert of a fallen world, to the eternal Promised Land of Heaven.

Jesus poured out his blood for us on the Cross. By his blood, we are saved from death. He is the eternal sacrificial Lamb, offered once in atonement for all of our sins. Jesus is the perfect unblemished Lamb, not sacrificed by another, but who freely sacrificed himself for us. As John proclaims in the Book of Revelation, we are invited to stand before the throne of God in Heaven with our clothes washed "white in the blood of the Lamb" (Rev 7:14).

In this story, we see again a prefiguration of Christian Baptism. Moses led the people through the water of the sea, from physical death at the hands of the Egyptian army to life in the Promised Land. Jesus leads us through the water of Baptism, from eternal death caused by sin to eternal life in Heaven.

Meditation 2: The Second Coming of Christ

The Passover and Exodus of the Israelites was not an end but a beginning. God brought his people out of slavery in Egypt and offered a new relationship with them — he would lead them and provide for their needs in the desert. The desert was not, however, their destination but merely a journey toward the land promised to them.

The coming of Jesus as man two thousand years ago was not an end but merely a new beginning. God entered into a new, more intimate relationship with us, his people. He instituted the sacraments by which all mankind might be saved. He showed us the path to Heaven. But we must walk that path.

We are in the same position the Israelites were in after crossing through the sea. We have been saved. We are being saved. And we will be saved, but only if we continue to journey with God, continue to grow close to him, continue to follow him, and continue to avail ourselves of the sacraments and the grace that he offers to us daily.

The First Coming of our Lord was a beginning. The Second Coming of our Lord is our end. Are you ready to set your sights on this end and go forth?

Meditation 3: The Third Coming of Christ

It is hard to let go of fear and live in trust. The Israelites were sick of the oppression of the Egyptians. But this slavery was a reality to which they had slowly become accustomed. To leave their slavery for a "Promised Land," "flowing with milk and honey," took trust. They had to trust that God would, through Moses, lead them out of Egypt, through the desert, and give them a land inhabited by a people hostile to them. They had to rely on promises made by God to others, e.g., Noah, Abraham, Jacob (Israel), and Moses. They had to trust that God would lead them and protect them from many very real dangers.

We face the same challenge in accepting the Third Coming of Christ. Jesus is truly present in our lives. He is concerned for us. He wants to guide us and guard us in our daily lives. He asks us to go in directions that are scary and to make decisions that have unknown outcomes. He asks us to ignore our fear and trust in him.

Even when we say yes and invite Jesus into our lives, not everything goes smoothly. Immediately after deciding to follow Moses, it looked to the Israelites that they would be massacred. But they were not. At the last second, in an unimaginable way, God provided for them.

Jesus is with us at every moment of every day. That does not mean we will always feel his presence. We won't. Nor does it mean that we will not experience pain and even death. Because of sin, we will. But, like the Israelites, God will ultimately bring us out of this earthly captivity, through the waters of death, and into our home with him.

How will you come to trust in God's loving providence? How will you embrace these five simple words: "Jesus, I trust in you!"

DECEMBER 14

Reading: God Provides in the Desert[1]

They set out from Elim, and all the congregation of the sons of Israel came to the wilderness of Sin, which is between Elim and Sinai, on the fifteenth day of the second month after they had departed from the land of Egypt. And the whole congregation of the sons of Israel murmured against Moses and Aaron in the wilderness, and said to them, "Would that we had died by the hand of the LORD in the land of Egypt, when we sat by the fleshpots and ate bread to the full; for you have brought us out into this wilderness to kill this whole assembly with hunger."

Then the LORD said to Moses, "Behold, I will rain bread from heaven for you; and the people shall go out and gather a day's portion every day, that I may test them, whether they will walk in my law or not. On the sixth day, when they prepare what they bring in, it will be twice as much as they gather daily." . . .

In the evening quails came up and covered the camp; and in the morning dew lay round about the camp. And when the dew had gone up, there was on the face of the wilderness a fine, flake-like thing, fine as hoarfrost on the ground. When the sons of Israel saw it, they said to one another, "What is it?" . . . And Moses said to them, "It is the bread which the LORD has given you to eat. This is what the LORD has commanded: 'Gather of it, every man of you, as much as he can eat.'" . . . And Moses said to them, "Let no man leave any of it till the morning." But they did not listen to

[1] Exodus 16:1–5, 13–16, 19–20, 22–24, 27–31; 17:1, 3, 5–7.

Moses; some left part of it till the morning, and it bred worms and became foul. . . .

On the sixth day they gathered twice as much bread. . . . [Moses] said to them, "This is what the LORD has commanded: 'Tomorrow is a day of solemn rest, a holy sabbath to the LORD; bake what you will bake and boil what you will boil, and all that is left over lay by to be kept till the morning.'" So they laid it by till the morning, as Moses bade them; and it did not become foul. . . . On the seventh day some of the people went out to gather, and they found none. And the LORD said to Moses, "How long do you refuse to keep my commandments and my laws? See! The LORD has given you the sabbath, therefore on the sixth day he gives you bread for two days; remain every man of you in his place, let no man go out of his place on the seventh day." So the people rested on the seventh day.

Now the house of Israel called its name manna; it was like coriander seed, white, and the taste of it was like wafers made with honey. . . .

All the congregation of the sons of Israel moved on from the wilderness of Sin . . . and camped at Rephidim; but there was no water for the people to drink. . . . The people murmured against Moses, and said, "Why did you bring us up out of Egypt, to kill us . . . with thirst?" . . . And the LORD said to Moses, "Pass on before the people, taking with you some of the elders of Israel; and take in your hand the rod with which you struck the Nile, and go. Behold, I will stand before you there on the rock at Horeb; and you shall strike the rock, and water shall come out of it, that the people may drink." And Moses did so, in the sight of the elders of Israel. And he called the name of the place Massah and Meribah, because of the fault-finding of the sons of Israel, and because they put the LORD to the test by saying, "Is the LORD among us or not?"

Meditation 1: The First Coming of Christ

The story of God providing manna in the desert is the harbinger of Jesus coming as man to give us the Eucharist. God "rained bread from heaven" in the form of manna as life-sustaining sustenance for the Israelites. Jesus is the "Bread from Heaven" who came down to provide the means of eternal life for all of us.

In their hunger, the people complained against Moses. They glorified the food of their slavery and failed to trust God's promise that they would be led safely into a land of abundance. On one level, this allowed God to show his constancy and to miraculously provide food and water. On a deeper level, this prepared his people for the eventual coming of the Messiah. Like Moses, Jesus miraculously fed the people (see Jn 6:25–27). Yet he pointed out the truth that no earthly food will ever satisfy, as hunger will always return. God did not want to provide food that merely satisfied the Israelites so as to avoid a rebellion against Moses. Similarly, God did not wish to provide food that merely satisfied the hungry crowd that was following Jesus. God provides for our temporal needs so as to woo us to receive that which will satisfy our supernatural needs. Food was merely a necessity in the desert that allowed the people to follow Moses and become a people set apart from others and dedicated to God. Food was merely a necessity so that the people would remain with Jesus and receive his life-giving words. The Eucharist would be the everlasting and ever-fulfilling food.

In predicting his gift of himself in the Eucharist, Jesus called to mind this very event in the desert and compared it to himself. "I am the bread of life. Your fathers ate the manna in the wilderness, and they died. This is the bread which comes down from heaven, that a man may eat of it and not die. I am the living bread which came down from heaven; if any one eats of this bread, he will live forever; and the bread which I shall give for the life of the world is my flesh" (Jn 6:48–51). It is no mere coincidence that the host, which we consecrate at Mass, is most commonly a "fine flake like thing." Like manna, the host is both familiar and mysterious. It looks like bread. It tastes like bread. Yet it is so much more. It is the very Body, Blood, Soul, and Divinity of our Lord. The bread that our Lord gives us to eat fills us with the very life of God, sustaining us not for an hour, a day, or even for years but for eternity. Can you accept that God loves you so much that he would offer himself up to be life-giving food for you? Do you truly believe in his Real Presence in the Eucharist?

Meditation 2: The Second Coming of Christ

Interwoven with this story is a reference to God's judgment. God is not our "wish granter" to whom we turn when we need something. God "provides" for us but also "requires" of us. God provided manna but required the people to trust him. He gave them one day's worth of food and asked them to trust that he would provide the next day's food. When they did not trust and collected more, the food rotted.

The rotting of the food is symbolic of the rotting of the peoples' hearts. Throughout the Exodus, God continually provided for the Israelites, yet it was never enough. They continually turned against Moses and God. They doubted. They disobeyed. And while God forgave and continued to provide, God ultimately allowed the consequences of the Israelites' choice against God. They suffered. They died. And most did not enter the Promised Land.

In the end, we will stand before God and be judged. We will either enter the eternal Promised Land or not. But it is important to remember that God is not a mean and vengeful God. The stories of "God's tests" in the Old Testament are not capricious but intentional and poignant. They are not really tests but lessons. We cannot provide for ourselves in any true way. We did not create ourselves, and we cannot sustain our lives. If God were to stop acting to animate our lives, we would cease to exist.

Despite our complete reliance upon God for existence, we are not created as mere automatons or puppets in God's hands. God created us to respond to him and to react in concert with him. God does not want us to choose good for his sake but for ours. He wants what is best for us but allows us to choose that which is not. This is free will. This is love. A parent who admonishes a child not to touch a hot stove does not do so for the parent's good or to test the child but because the parent desires the good of the child. God admonished the people not to rely on their own provision to teach them the truth that only he could provide for their true needs.

Choosing the good over the bad is not easy. God knows this and will be merciful at our Final Judgment. But he will also be just. If we continually choose our own distorted will over God's, he will allow us the fruit of our imperfect, disordered will. He will allow us to exist in ourselves, separated from him. Are you relying on your own efforts to get you through this life? Are you trying to merit Heaven? Do you think Heaven is something to be obtained, rather than a gift to be received from your loving Father?

Meditation 3: The Third Coming of Christ

The lesson of this passage for us is to live in the "now." Jesus comes to us today, right where were are. We are never absent in God's mind and heart. He is never unconcerned for us. God is not the God of yesterday or tomorrow. He does not meet us in our history or in our future. He meets us in every moment, as we live it. If we wish to encounter God and receive his blessing, we must do so by living in the present, releasing our past, and entrusting our future to him.

In the only prayer Jesus gave us, he admonishes us to ask for our "daily bread," not for a stockpile of bread to sustain us in the future. When he fed the thousands with the loaves and fishes, Jesus provided just enough for them to remain in his presence that day to receive his life-giving words. Jesus comes to us today and asks us to trust that he will provide just what we need today. When tomorrow becomes today, he will extend the same invitation.

We must also remember that God offers to provide not what we perceive we need but what he knows to be best for us. The Israelites pined for the fleshpots of their slavery in Egypt. God offered them something better, even if they did not realize at the time that it was better.

Every day, Christ confronts us personally. He invites us to walk alongside him. And he offers to fill us with the very bread of salvation — his Body, Blood, Soul, and Divinity in the Eucharist.

> "Therefore I tell you, do not be anxious about your life, what you shall eat or what you shall drink, nor about your body, what you shall put on. . . . Look at the birds of the air: they neither sow nor reap nor gather into barns, and yet your heavenly Father feeds them. Are you not of more value than they? . . . Therefore do not be anxious, saying, 'What shall we eat?' or 'What shall we drink?' or 'What shall we wear? . . . Do not be anxious about tomorrow, for tomorrow will be anxious for itself. Let the day's own trouble be sufficient for the day."
>
> — Matthew 6:25–26, 31, 34

Will you seek to forget about yesterday, not worry about tomorrow, and live today with God?

DECEMBER 15

Reading: God Gives the Ten Commandments[1]

On the third new moon after the sons of Israel had gone forth out of the land of Egypt, on that day they came into the wilderness of Sinai. . . . And there Israel encamped before the mountain. . . .

On the morning of the third day there was thunder and lightning, and a thick cloud upon the mountain, and a very loud trumpet blast. . . . And the LORD came down upon Mount Sinai, to the top of the mountain; and the LORD called Moses to the top of the mountain, and Moses went up.

And God spoke all these words, saying,

"I am the LORD your God, who brought you out of the land of Egypt, out of the house of bondage.

"You shall have no other gods before me.

"You shall not make for yourself a graven image, or any likeness of anything that is in heaven above, or that is in the earth beneath, or that is in the water under the earth; you shall not bow down to them or serve them; for I the LORD your God am a jealous God, visiting the iniquity of the fathers upon the children to the third and the fourth generation of those who hate me, but showing mercy to thousands of those who love me and keep my commandments.

"You shall not take the name of the LORD your God in vain; for the LORD will not hold him guiltless who takes his name in vain.

"Remember the sabbath day, to keep it holy. Six days you shall labor, and do all your work; but the seventh day is a sabbath to the LORD your God; in it you shall not do any work, you, or

[1]   Exodus 19:1–2, 16, 20; 20:1–17.

your son, or your daughter, your manservant, or your maidservant, or your cattle, or the sojourner who is within your gates; for in six days the LORD made heaven and earth, the sea, and all that is in them, and rested the seventh day; therefore the LORD blessed the sabbath day and hallowed it.

"Honor your father and your mother, that your days may be long in the land which the LORD your God gives you.

"You shall not kill.

"You shall not commit adultery.

"You shall not steal.

"You shall not bear false witness against your neighbor.

"You shall not covet your neighbor's house; you shall not covet your neighbor's wife, or his manservant, or his maidservant, or his ox, or his donkey, or anything that is your neighbor's."

Meditation 1: The First Coming of Christ

It is no mere coincidence that the Lord came down upon Mount Sinai on the "morning of the third day" (Ex 19:16). This coming down of the Lord to give the Ten Commandments is referred to as the Great Theophany (the great revealing by God of himself to his people). This event prefigures the second Great Theophany — that of Jesus on Easter morning. On the morning of the third day (following his death), Christ revealed himself resurrected and glorified.

On Mount Sinai, God revealed his existence with great signs, appearing in a personal way to Moses. God revealed his love for his people by setting them apart from all others as a people who were God's own, providing them a blueprint on how to live a good and holy life. On Easter morning, Jesus revealed to the Apostles and others his divinity in a definitive way — he rose from the dead. Jesus revealed his love by suffering and dying for all men and women, by conquering death, paying the price for the sin of Adam and Eve, and opening the gates of Heaven for us all.

The Law given by God to us through Moses prefigured the New Law given to us by Jesus. The Old Law was for a people who were spiritual children. It spelled out specific action — what to do and what not to do. The Law of Jesus did not negate this first Law but fulfilled and perfected it. When we had traveled with God for many years, through times of love and obedience to him and times of rebellion from him, God found us ready to come closer to him and more perfectly conform ourselves to him.

The Old Law admonished us to love God and to love our neighbor. The New Law invites us to love our neighbor as ourselves, to love our enemies and pray for our persecutors, and to love God to the point of complete sacrifice of ourselves. The Old Law was one of rules aimed at teaching right action that would lead to a conformity of will and heart. The New Law is an invitation first to love and then to conform our wills to that love. When Christ came two thousand years ago, he addressed us not as slaves ransomed from Egypt but as sons and daughters who were ready to embrace their Father freely.

Meditation 2: The Second Coming of Christ

"On the morning of the third day there were thunders and lightning, and a thick cloud upon the mountain, and a very loud trumpet blast. . . . And the LORD came down upon Mount Sinai, to the top of the mountain" (Ex 19:16, 20). This dramatic image of God coming down upon Mount Sinai is evocative of the image offered in the Book of Revelation regarding the Second Coming of Christ. Following the seventh trumpet blast, there were "flashes of lightning, voices, peals of thunder" (Rev 11:19), and God's Temple in Heaven was revealed. Thereafter, the Spirit carried the writer to a great, high mountain and showed him the New Jerusalem coming down from Heaven (see Rev 21:10).

The old Jerusalem, into which Jesus entered on Palm Sunday as its king, was on the same mountain on which God came down to Moses. God came down upon the mountain of Sinai and gave his "words" — the Ten Commandments (also referred to as the Decalogue or "Ten Words") — to dwell with his people. In Christ, God came down upon the mountain of Jerusalem in the Person of "the Word" (see Jn 1) to dwell bodily with his people (in the form of his physical body for thirty years and, thereafter, in the form of his Body, Blood, Soul, and Divinity present in the Eucharist). At the end of time, God will come down again, not to an existing and imperfect mountain, but in the form of the true and everlasting holy mountain of Jerusalem in which he and his people will dwell together for all eternity.

God revealed himself to Moses on Mount Sinai as "the LORD your God, who brought you out of the land of Egypt, out of the house of bondage" (Ex 20:2). At the Second Coming, God will reveal himself to each of us as the Lord our God who has brought us out of our bondage to sin and death. Those who have lived the Law of Love and have loved God and loved their neighbor as themselves, God will invite to remain with him forever on top of the mountain. How can you better prepare yourself for his coming? How can you better live the law of love?

Meditation 3: The Third Coming of Christ

We are so blessed to be living every day in the Third Coming of Christ. God is truly and intimately present in our lives at every moment of every day. God is not isolated from us, high upon a mountain and clouded in smoke. The Spirit of God dwells within us from our Baptism. We partake in Christ's Body, Blood, Soul, and Divinity in the Eucharist. We can gaze upon the Real Presence of God in an Adoration chapel.

Through Moses, God called for the observance of the Sabbath on the seventh day. As Christ pointed out, this was not a burden placed upon mankind but a gift of God. Man was not made for the Sabbath, but the Sabbath was made for man. The Sabbath was given as a day of worship and rest. It is important for us to observe the Sabbath — to recognize God's presence, to let go of our works and worries, and to allow God to bless us and refresh us. Worship of our Lord on the Sabbath should never be a burden. We go to Mass on Sunday to bend our knees and adore the Lord and to thank him for all the wondrous things he has done for us. And he comes to dwell within us in the most intimate way.

In the beginning, the Sabbath was prefigured in the story of creation. On the seventh day, having completed his creative work, God "rested" and blessed this seventh day. At the First Coming of Christ, the people of God observed the seventh day by literally resting and worshiping God as proscribed by God through Moses. But Christ perfected the Sabbath and made all things new (see Rev 21:5). In him began a new creation — an eighth day — the day of the Resurrection. We especially observe this new day of Sabbath, this eighth day, on Sunday (even referring to every Sunday as a "little Easter"). But we are also called to live every day as the eighth day. All things are new in Christ. We are reborn in water and Spirit. We live in the redemption of Christ and the hope of Heaven. Every day, we are to call out in the words of St. Paul (and the proclamation of the Advent Season) — "Maranâ thâ," "Our Lord, come!" (1 Cor 16:22).

While every day is to be one of lived encounter, this is especially true of Sunday. Do you "honor the Sabbath"? Do you rest? Do you stop "doing" and allow yourself to "receive"?

DECEMBER 16

Reading: Entry into the Promised Land; Joshua and the Battle of Jericho[1]

After the death of Moses, . . . the LORD said to Joshua, . . . Moses' minister, ". . . Go over this Jordan, you and all this people, into the land which I am giving to them, to the sons of Israel. . . . Only be strong and very courageous, being careful to do according to all the law which Moses my servant commanded you." . . .

Early in the morning Joshua rose and set out from Shittim, with all the sons of Israel; and they came to the Jordan. . . .

And the LORD said to Joshua, "This day I will begin to exalt you in the sight of all Israel, that they may know that, as I was with Moses, so I will be with you. And you shall command the priests who bear the ark of the covenant, 'When you come to the brink of the waters of the Jordan, you shall stand still in the Jordan.'" . . .

When those who bore the ark had come to the Jordan, and the feet of the priests bearing the ark were dipped in the brink of the water, . . . the waters coming down from above stood and rose up in a heap far off, . . . and those flowing down toward the sea . . . were wholly cut off; and the people passed over opposite Jericho. . . .

And when the priests bearing the ark . . . came up from the midst of the Jordan, and the soles of the priests' feet were lifted up on dry ground, the waters of the Jordan returned to their place and overflowed all its banks, as before. . . .

Now Jericho was shut up from within and from without because of the sons of Israel; none went out, and none came in. And

[1] Joshua 1:1–2, 7; 3:1, 7–8, 15–16; 4:18; 6:1–5, 15–17, 20.

the LORD said to Joshua, "See, I have given into your hand Jericho, with its king and mighty men of valor. You shall march around the city, all the men of war going around the city once. Thus shall you do for six days. And seven priests shall bear seven trumpets of rams' horns before the ark; and on the seventh day you shall march around the city seven times, the priests blowing the trumpets. And when they make a long blast with the ram's horn, as soon as you hear the sound of the trumpet, then all the people shall shout with a great shout; and the wall of the city will fall down flat, and the people shall go up every man straight before him." . . .

On the seventh day they rose early at the dawn of day, and marched around the city in the same manner seven times: it was only on that day that they marched around the city seven times. And at the seventh time, when the priests had blown the trumpets, Joshua said to the people, "Shout; for the LORD has given you the city." . . . As soon as the people heard the sound of the trumpet, the people raised a great shout, and the wall fell down flat, so that the people went up into the city, every man straight before him, and they took the city.

Meditation 1: The First Coming of Christ

Joshua is one of the most overt prefigurements of Christ. The names "Joshua" and "Jesus" are merely two forms of the same name (the name "Jesus" is derived from Yeshua, which is a shortened form of Joshua or Yehoshua). The name means to "save" or "deliver" — the preeminent action of both Joshua and Jesus.

Joshua was the instrument of God by which the Israelites were finally freed of their slavery in Egypt and their wandering in the desert. Jesus was the instrument of God (and God Incarnate) by which all people are freed from the slavery of sin, death, and the sojourn here on earth.

Joshua led the people safely through the waters of the Jordan River into the Promised Land. Reentering into the Jorden River and submitting to the baptism of John, Jesus instituted the Christian Sacrament of Baptism, the means by which all might enter the true and eternal "promised land" of Heaven. Just as the Israelites followed Joshua through the water into a new life in the Promised Land, we are invited to follow Jesus through the waters of Baptism into new life as sons and daughters of God with an ultimate destination of Heaven.

For seven days, Joshua and the Israelites walked before the walls of Jericho. On the seventh day, through God's power, the walls fell, and the Promised Land was opened to the people. On the eighth day, they began their days in the Promised Land under the leadership of Joshua. Jesus and his disciples approached the walls of Jerusalem. On the seventh day, through Jesus' Resurrection, the walls separating God from man fell. The sin of Adam was expiated. Death was overcome. The gates of Heaven were flung open. Christ instituted the new "eighth day," following the "seventh day" of the Sabbath, from whence we have begun the new age, not under the leadership of the man Joshua, but under Jesus, who is God Incarnate.

Meditation 2: The Second Coming of Christ

If we are honest with ourselves, we will admit that we are just like the Israelites. God has done so much for us, but we are "hard-hearted" and "stiff-necked." We constantly turn away from God. We constantly sin. When facing the reality that we will die one day and stand before God, with all of our sins and failings laid bare, we might despair greatly. We might fear that we are unworthy of Heaven.

Such fear is unfounded. Of course, we should strive to love God with our whole heart, soul, mind, and strength and our neighbor as ourselves. Of course, this love should produce good actions in us. But we will never be "worthy" of Heaven. We will never merit Heaven. We cannot merit Heaven. But we do not need to merit Heaven. Heaven has already been won for us by Jesus.

We must not fear our imperfections. We must recognize them and surrender them to God in prayer and in the Sacrament of Confession. We must boldly call upon the mercy of God poured out in Baptism, Reconciliation, and the Holy Eucharist. Mindful of God's justice, we must rely on God's mercy.

Jesus is the perfect Lamb that has been offered as reparation for all our sins. Jesus has paid the debt owed to God for all the sins of all mankind for all times. At the Final Judgment, the horns spoken of in the Book of Revelation will join those of the horns of Jericho, and the walls separating us from God will fall. As the Israelites followed Joshua into the Promised Land, we who have said yes to God's love and grace will joyfully follow Jesus into the heavenly Jerusalem. How can you better embrace God's salvation in a new, more intimate way? What lie stands in the way of accepting the fact that God loves you and wants you to live with him for all eternity?

Meditation 3: The Third Coming of Christ

"Be strong and very courageous, being careful to do according to all the law which Moses my servant commanded you" (Jos 1:7). This admonition applies equally to us as it did to the Israelites. Remember Jesus' words that he came not to abolish but to fulfill the Law.

We are blessed to live in the fulfillment of the Law. We do not blindly follow rules (some of which may seem arbitrary). Rather, we are called to come to an understanding of the proper relationship between God, ourselves, and our neighbor. We are called not merely to refrain from offending God and our neighbor but to actively seek to love God and our neighbor (even our enemy).

Through mighty deeds, God sought to assure his people that he was "with Moses" and was "with Joshua" in order that the people would listen to their instructions and heed their teachings. God continues to provide us with guidance through his chosen spokesmen — the pope, bishops, and priests. The mightiest of deeds are accomplished daily through their hands — bread and wine are transubstantiated into the Body, Blood, Soul, and Divinity of Jesus. Through the words of the priest, "I absolve you," God completely forgives us of all our sins contritely confessed. The pope, in union with the bishops, speaks infallibly upon matters of faith and morals.

Priests are not perfect, nor were Moses or Joshua. But God worked through his unworthy servants Moses and Joshua and continues to work through his priests and bishops (despite their many failings). How can you better listen to God's words spoken to you through his priests to discern what God is saying to you and asking you to do? How can you better humble yourself, not before a human priest, but to God acting through his priest?

DECEMBER 17

Reading: Kingship — Saul and the Anointing of David[1]

Samuel grew, and the LORD was with him. . . . And all Israel . . . knew that Samuel was established as a prophet of the LORD.

Samuel judged Israel all the days of his life. . . .

Then all the elders of Israel gathered together and came to Samuel at Ramah, and said to him, "Behold, you are old and your sons do not walk in your ways; now appoint for us a king to govern us like all the nations." . . .

And the LORD said to Samuel, ". . . They have rejected me from being king over them. According to all the deeds which they have done to me, from the day I brought them up out of Egypt even to this day, forsaking me and serving other gods. Now then, . . . you shall solemnly warn them, and show them the ways of the king who shall reign over them." . . .

But the people refused to listen to the voice of Samuel. . . . And the LORD said to Samuel, "Listen to their voice, and make them a king." . . .

There was a man of Benjamin whose name was Kish, . . . a Benjaminite, a man of wealth; and he had a son whose name was Saul, a handsome young man. There was not a man among the sons of Israel more handsome than he; from his shoulders upward he was taller than any of the people. . . .

Samuel took a vial of oil and poured it on his head, and kissed him and said, "Has not the LORD anointed you to be prince over

---

[1] 1 Samuel 3:19–20; 7:15; 8:4–5, 7–9, 19, 22; 9:1–2; 10:1; 14:47–48; 15:1–3, 7, 9–11; 16:1, 4–7, 10–13.

his people Israel? And you shall reign over the people of the Lord and you will save them from the hand of their enemies." . . .

When Saul had taken the kingship over Israel, he fought against all his enemies on every side; . . . wherever he turned he put them to the worse. And he did valiantly . . . and delivered Israel out of the hands of those who plundered them. . . .

And Samuel said to Saul, ". . . Thus says the Lord of hosts, 'I will punish what Am'alek did to Israel in opposing them on the way, when they came up out of Egypt. Now go and strike Am'alek, and utterly destroy all that they have; do not spare them, but kill both man and woman, infant and suckling, ox and sheep, camel and donkey.'" . . .

And Saul defeated the Amal'ekites. . . . But Saul and the people spared A'gag, and the best of the sheep and of the oxen and of the fatlings, and the lambs, and all that was good, and would not utterly destroy them; all that was despised and worthless they utterly destroyed. . . .

The word of the Lord came to Samuel: "I repent that I have made Saul king; for he has turned back from following me, and has not performed my commandments." . . .

The Lord said to Samuel, ". . . Fill your horn with oil, and go; I will send you to Jesse the Bethlehemite, for I have provided for myself a king among his sons." . . . Samuel did what the Lord commanded, and came to Bethlehem. . . . And he said, "Peaceably; I have come to sacrifice to the Lord; consecrate yourselves, and come with me to the sacrifice." And he consecrated Jesse and his sons, and invited them to the sacrifice.

When they came, he looked on Eli'ab and thought, "Surely the Lord's anointed is before him." But the Lord said to Samuel, "Do not look on his appearance or on the height of his stature, because I have rejected him; for the Lord sees not as man sees; man looks on the outward appearance, but the Lord looks on the heart." . . . And Jesse made seven of his sons pass before Samuel. And Samuel said to Jesse, "The LORD has not chosen these." And Samuel said to Jesse, "Are all your sons here?" And he said, "There remains yet the youngest, but behold, he is keeping the sheep." And Samuel said to Jesse, "Send and fetch him." . . . And he sent, and brought him in. Now he was ruddy, and had beautiful eyes, and was handsome. And the LORD said, "Arise, anoint him; for this is he." Then Samuel took the horn of oil, and anointed him in the midst of his brothers; and the Spirit of the LORD came mightily upon David from that day forward.

Meditation 1: The First Coming of Christ

The anointing of a king foreshadows the coming of the one true king, Jesus. Jesus would not be merely a decent king like Saul, who was at first loyal to God but then turned away. Nor would he be even like the great King David, who failed in many ways but remained steadfast in his love of God and repented of all of his failings. Jesus, as true God and true man, would be the perfect king.

The failures of Saul's reign point to the perfections of Jesus' kingship. Saul (as we learn in other verses of Scripture) was arrogant and jealous. His kingly glory resided in his conquest in battle. Jesus was humble and completely self-sacrificing. His kingly glory resided in his perfect obedience to the will of the Father and his complete self-abandonment for the good of all.

According to human standards, Saul seemed to be a far better candidate for king than David. David was the youngest of his brothers and seemingly an afterthought by his own father. He was a mere shepherd from an unimportant town. But, as pointed out in this passage, "the LORD sees not as man sees; man looks on the outward appearance, but the LORD looks on the heart" (1 Sm 16:7). David, not Saul, most closely reflected Jesus.

David was from a family of Bethlehem. Thereafter, the prophet Micah foretold that the Messiah (and true king) would also come from Bethlehem. "But you, O Bethlehem Ephˈrathah, who are little to be among the clans of Judah, from you shall come forth for me one who is to be ruler in Israel whose origin is from of old, from ancient days" (Mi 5:2). In fulfillment of this prophecy, Jesus, like David, was born in Bethlehem. Like David, Jesus was, from outward appearances, the least likely to be a king. His father was a mere carpenter. He lived in Nazareth and was the object of prejudices against Nazareth. In the words of Phillip, "can anything good come out of Nazareth?" (Jn 1:46). David was a shepherd, and Jesus the Good Shepherd.

That God brings forth greatness from the unexpected can be seen in the prophetic word of Isaiah predicting that the Messiah would not be an arrogant autocrat but a suffering servant: "He had no form or comeliness that we should look at him, and no beauty that we should desire him. He was despised and rejected by men; a man of sorrows, and acquainted with grief; . . . he was despised, and we esteemed him not" (Is 53:2–3).

Meditation 2: The Second Coming of Christ

This passage chosen for today very much compresses the story of King Saul found in Bible. Saul did many mighty deeds and accomplished great feats in the name of the Lord. Yet, as we see here, he was ultimately rejected by God, and a young man from "nowhere" was chosen in his stead. Mindful of the Second Coming of Christ, we are challenged to examine ourselves. We desire to be chosen like David rather than rejected like Saul.

Call to mind the cautionary words of Jesus, "Not every one who says to me, 'Lord, Lord,' shall enter the kingdom of heaven, but he who does the will of my Father who is in heaven. On that day many will say to me, 'Lord, Lord, did we not prophesy in your name, and cast out demons in your name, and do many mighty works in your name?' And then will I declare to them, 'I never knew you; depart from me, you evildoers'" (Mt 7:21–23). Great deeds are not the measure of a man or woman. Rather, even the smallest deed done with great love is what is desired by God.

Outwardly, it looked like Saul was obedient to God. In reality, he was arrogant and self-serving. God, not Saul, was the victor over his many enemies. God allowed Saul to benefit greatly from his victories. Yet, when God asked for all of Saul's love and obedience, Saul was not prepared to give this. As we learn when we read his story, David was a man who was just as broken and just as much a sinner as Saul. David, however, loved God with an amazing love. David regretted his sins. David humbled himself and asked pardon from God. David, ultimately, sought to give glory to God above his own interests.

Very few of us will live a life that stands out for obvious greatness. That is fine and, maybe, even a blessing for our humility. Every one of us can, however, live lives of love — toward God, our neighbor, and ourselves. We will not earn Heaven by great works, but, if we approach the throne after a lifelong love affair with God, we will hear the words, "Come, O blessed of my Father, inherit the kingdom prepared for you from the foundation of the world" (Mt 25:34). Is there an area of pride in your life that is distancing you from God? Is there someone in your life whom you are called to love better?

Meditation 3: The Third Coming of Christ

This story is replete with instances of God coming to his people in the present moment, seeking to interact with them, to teach them, and to guide them. It underlines our freedom of how we will respond to God's interaction.

God came to Samuel. He assured Samuel that, in their request for a king, the people were not so much rejecting Samuel after his many years of leadership as they were rejecting God, who had been the source of Samuel's leadership. Samuel humbled himself before the Lord and the people and did as the Lord asked, anointing Saul as king.

God came to the people through Samuel. He warned them that their desire to have a king, like all the pagan nations of the earth, was a disordered desire that would bring very bad consequences (if you read all of the stories of the kings that follow, you will learn that the kingship was, in great part, disastrous for the Israelites). The people ignored God's warning and received the bad consequences.

God came to Saul and, in return for yet another victory in battle, requested obedience from Saul. Saul disobeyed God and kept the spoils of war. Because of this, God stripped the kingship from Saul.

Last in this story is the coming of God to David. David was anointed, and the Spirit of the Lord came upon him. The story ends with anticipation — will David listen to and obey God and receive God's continued blessings?

Today, we are in the same place as David at the end of this story. Through our Baptism (and Confirmation), we have been anointed by God in even a more powerful way than David. We have been recreated and adopted as children of God. The Holy Spirit dwells within us. Every day, Christ comes to us personally in both the big and small happenings of our lives. He wishes to be a part of them all. He wishes to be the inspiration for all decisions. He wants to walk with us through the good and bad — to teach us, guide us, laugh with us, console us, bless us, and bring us to the eternal house of his Father. How will you respond?

DECEMBER 18

Reading: The Kingship of David[1]

David arose and went . . . to bring up from there the ark of God . . .
out of the house of Abinadab which was on a hill . . . to the city
of David with rejoicing; and when those who bore the ark of the
LORD had gone six paces, he sacrificed an ox and a fatling. And
David danced before the LORD with all his might. . . .

The king said to Nathan the prophet, "See now, I dwell in a
house of cedar, but the ark of God dwells in a tent." And Nathan
said to the king, "Go do all that is in your heart; for the LORD is
with you."

But that same night the word of the LORD came to Nathan,
"Go and tell my servant David, 'Thus says the LORD: . . . When
your days are fulfilled and you lie down with your fathers, I will
raise up your offspring after you, who shall come forth from your
body, and I will establish his kingdom. He shall build a house for
my name, and I will establish the throne of his kingdom forever. . . .
When he commits iniquity, I will chasten him with the rod of men,
with the stripes of the sons of men; but I will not take my merciful love from him, as I took it from Saul, whom I put away from
before you. And your house and your kingdom shall be made sure
for ever before me; your throne shall be established for ever.'"

In the spring of the year, the time when kings go forth to battle, David sent Jo'ab, and his servants with him, and all Israel; and
they ravaged the Am'monites, and besieged Rabbah. But David
remained in Jerusalem.

[1] 2 Samuel 6:2–3, 12–14; 7:2–5, 12–16; 11:1–6, 8, 11, 14–15, 26–27; 12:1, 7, 9,
13–16, 18, 20, 24.

It happened, late one afternoon, when David arose from his couch and was walking upon the roof of the king's house, that he saw from the roof a woman bathing; and the woman was very beautiful. And David sent and inquired about the woman. And one said, "Is this not Bathshe'ba, . . . the wife of Uri'ah the Hittite?" So David sent messengers, and took her; . . . and he lay with her. . . . And the woman conceived. . . .

So David sent word to Jo'ab, "Send me Uri'ah." . . . Then David said to Uri'ah, "Go down to your house." . . . Uri'ah said to David, "The ark and Israel . . . dwell in booths; and my lord Jo'ab and the servants of my lord are camping in the open field; shall I then go to my house, to eat and drink, and to lie with my wife? . . . I will not do this thing." . . .

In the morning David wrote a letter to Jo'ab, . . . "Set Uri'ah in the forefront of the hardest fighting, and then draw back from him, that he may be struck down and die." . . .

When the wife of Uri'ah heard that Uriah was dead, she made lamentation for her husband. And when the morning was over, David sent and brought her to his house, and she became his wife, and bore him a son. . . .

The LORD sent Nathan to David. . . . "Thus says the LORD, the God of Israel, 'I anointed you king over Israel, and I delivered you out of the hand of Saul. . . . Why have you despised the word of the LORD, to do what is evil in his sight?'" . . . David said to Nathan, "I have sinned against the LORD." And Nathan said to David, "The LORD has put away your sin; you shall not die. Nevertheless, . . . the child that is born to you shall die." . . .

And the LORD struck the child. . . . David therefore besought God for the child; and fasted, and went in and lay all night upon the ground. . . On the seventh day, the child died. . . . David arose from the earth, and washed, and anointed himself, and changed his clothes; and he went into the house of the LORD and worshiped. . . .Then David comforted his wife, Bathshe'ba, and went in to her, and lay with her; and she bore a son, and he called his name Solomon.

Meditation 1: The First Coming of Christ

This passage begins with King David escorting the Ark of the Covenant into his city. The Ark was the physical representation of God dwelling with his people. It contained the words of God — the stone tablets upon which God wrote the Ten Commandments. It also contained manna from the desert.

David encounters the Ark of the Covenant in the hill country of Judea. He dances/leaps before the Ark of the Lord with joy. This prefigures the first encounter of John the Baptist with Jesus. John, still in his mother's womb, encounters Jesus in the hill country of Judea at the Visitation by Mary to Elizabeth. Just as David leaped with joy at the recognition of the presence of God within the man-made Ark, John (even before he is born) leaps with joy at the recognition of the true Presence of God within the divine-made Ark — the womb of the Virgin Mary (see Lk 1:41).

David is told by God through the words of Nathan that not David but his offspring would build the house of God. In one sense, this is fulfilled by David's son Solomon, who builds the first Temple. In a more poignant way, however, this is fulfilled by Jesus, who would be born of David's lineage. Jesus would not build a house of wood or stone to contain God's veiled presence in one location. Rather, Jesus himself is the Temple, and, through the Church that he would institute, which is the living Body of Christ throughout the world, God would dwell intimately with his people. Further, in instituting the Eucharist, Jesus provided for his Real Presence to dwell physically in every Tabernacle in every church throughout the world.

God also promised that, through David's offspring, an ever-lasting kingdom would be established. Following David, his descendants were sometimes good but mostly bad kings. Their kingdoms rose and fell. But Jesus is the King of Kings and the Lord of Lords. His is the everlasting Kingdom that reaches down from Heaven to earth and unites the temporal with the eternal.

This passage foretells of God's justice and mercy. "When he commits iniquity, I will chasten him with the rod of men, with the stripes of the sons of men; but I will not take my steadfast love from him, as I took it from Saul, whom I put away from before you." (2 Sm 7:14–15). In one way, this is fulfilled in Solomon (and even in the life of David himself). Both sin against God, and God allows them to suffer at the hands of others. But God is merciful and sustains them and their reign. In order to expiate the sins of all people of all times (including the sins of David and his off-spring), Jesus subjected himself to the chastening of men. In his scourging, Jesus received the chastening stripes deserved by us, and, in taking upon himself our guilt, he poured out God's mercy in return. In the words of the prophet Isaiah, "With his stripes we are healed" (Is 53:5).

Meditation 2: The Second Coming of Christ

The city of David points both to the Jerusalem of old and the new "heavenly Jerusalem" of the future. In the past, God dwelt among his people shrouded in mystery. He revealed himself in symbols such as the manna, the king, and the Ark and dwelt in the Temple made by man in the form of a cloud. Then, God dwelt with us physically. The Second Person of the Blessed Trinity became Incarnate — "The Word became flesh and dwelt among us" (Jn 1:14). Entering Jerusalem, Jesus revealed that his body was the new Temple not made by man, which would be destroyed by man but then rebuilt by his own power (see Jn 2:19). As the Temple is no longer a particular building but the very Person of Jesus, the Temple is present everywhere. God dwells personally in the form of the Eucharist and in the priest who acts in the Person of Christ in administering the sacraments.

Christ's coming as the new Temple was not an end in itself but points to the future: "For here we have no lasting city, but seek the city that is to come" (Heb 13:14). The new Temple of our Lord's Body is not fully experienced by us here in our current state, where we remain subject to sin and not in full union with God. We read in the Book of Revelation that, at the Second Coming of Christ, the New Jerusalem will come down from Heaven to dwell here on earth (see Rev 21:2). In the Jerusalem that we call Heaven, there will be no separation between us and God. We will see him not as "in a mirror dimly" but "face to face," and we will understand him fully (1 Cor 13:12).

David wished to dwell with the Lord, and so should we. God dwells in us through grace. By our Baptism, we have become adopted children of the Father. In the Holy Eucharist, we receive the Body, Blood, Soul, and Divinity of Jesus. But we should desire even more — perfect union with our loving Triune God in Heaven. Looking not back to the Christmas of two thousand years ago but forward to the Second Coming, let us cry out, "Come, Lord Jesus!" (Rev 22:20). Do you actually think about Heaven from time to time? Do you truly desire Heaven?

Meditation 3: The Third Coming of Christ

At the heart of the beginning of the story is the desire of all men for our Lord to dwell with us personally and intimately. In the story of the Exodus, God dwelt imperfectly in a tent (or Tabernacle — the words can be used interchangeably). Both the Ark of the Covenant, which was kept in this tent, and the pillar of cloud that descended upon the tent when Moses entered signified the special presence of God with his people (see Ex 33 and 38). David wished to replace the tent with a glorious building of stone, cedar, gold, silver, and other precious metals. David desired that the Lord dwell within his city, close to his palace. Ultimately, this Temple was built by David's son Solomon.

By his institution of the Eucharist, Jesus has forever made himself far more accessible. God no longer dwells imperfectly within a single tent or Temple into which only a few privileged people (Moses, the priests, etc.) may enter. Rather, Jesus is truly and fully present — Body, Blood, Soul, and Divinity — in all the Tabernacles in all the churches throughout the world.

Even more powerful and personal than Jesus' dwelling within the Tabernacles of our churches is his dwelling within each of us. We are all "tabernacles" containing Jesus. All are called to come to the Eucharistic feast and receive God personally into our bodies and souls. We are to eat his flesh and drink his blood and, in doing so, Christ is in us, and we are in him (see Jn 6:54–56). How can you come to better embrace the reality that God unites himself to you in the Eucharist?

DECEMBER 19

Reading: King Solomon and the Temple[1]

At Gib'eon the LORD appeared to Solomon in a dream by night;
and God said, "Ask what I shall give you." And Solomon said, ". . .
O LORD my God, you have made your servant king in place of
David my father, although I am but a little child. . . . Give your
servant therefore an understanding mind to govern your people,
that I may discern between good and evil." . . .

And God said to him, "Because you have asked this, and have
not asked for yourself long life or riches or the life of your enemies, but have asked for yourself understanding to discern what is
right, behold, I now do according to your word. Behold, I give you
a wise and discerning mind, so that none like you has been before
you and none like you shall arise after you. I give you also what
you have not asked, both riches and honor, so that no other king
shall compare with you, all your days. And if you will walk in my
ways, keeping my statutes and my commandments, as your father
David walked, then I will lengthen your days." . . .

[Solomon] had dominion over all the region west of the
Euphra'tes from Tiphsah to Gaza, over all the kings west of the
Euphrates; and he had peace on all sides round about him. And
Judah and Israel dwelt in safety . . . all the days of Solomon. . . .

And God gave Solomon wisdom and understanding beyond
measure, and largeness of mind like the sand on the seashore, so
that Solomon's wisdom surpassed the wisdom of all the people of
the east, and all the wisdom of Egypt. . . . And men came from all

[1] 1 Kings 3:5, 7, 9, 11–14; 4:24–25, 29–30, 34; 5:2–5; 6:1, 11–15, 22; 8:1, 6,
10–11.

peoples to hear the wisdom of Solomon, and from all the kings of the earth, who had heard of his wisdom. . . .

And Solomon sent word to Hiram, "You know that David my father could not build a house for the name of the LORD his God because of the warfare with which his enemies surrounded him, until the LORD put them under the soles of his feet. But now the LORD my God has given me rest on every side; there is neither adversary nor misfortune. And so I purpose to build a house for the name of the LORD my God, as the LORD said to David my father, 'Your son, whom I will set upon your throne in your place, shall build the house for my name.'" . . .

In the four hundred and eightieth year after the sons of Israel came out of the land of Egypt, in the fourth year of Solomon's reign over Israel, . . . he began to build the house of the LORD. . . .

Now the word of the LORD came to Solomon, "Concerning this house which you are building, if you will walk in my statutes and obey my ordinances and keep all my commandments and walk in them, then I will establish my word with you, which I spoke to David your father. And I will dwell among the children of Israel, and will not forsake my people Israel."

So Solomon built the house, and finished it. He lined the walls of the house on the inside with boards of cedar. . . . He covered the floor of the house with boards of cypress. . . . And he overlaid the whole house with gold. . . .

Then Solomon assembled the elders of Israel and all the heads of the tribes, the leaders of the fathers' houses of the sons of Israel. . . . Then the priests brought the ark of the covenant of the LORD to its place, in the inner sanctuary of the house. . . . And when the priests came out of the holy place, a cloud filled the house of the LORD, so that the priests could not stand to minister because of the cloud; for the glory of the LORD filled the house of the LORD.

Meditation 1: The First Coming of Christ

Jesus is the perfection of the peace of Solomon. The reigns of David and the kings that followed Solomon were all marked with constant warfare. Only Solomon's reign was primarily filled with peace. In this, Solomon points to the coming of Christ. That the Messiah, like Solomon, would be a peaceful ruler is specifically predicted by the prophet Isaiah, "For to us a child is born ... and his name will be called ... Prince of Peace" (Is 9:6). We joyfully proclaim in the Christmas Liturgy, "In the forty-second year of the reign of Octavian Augustus, the whole world being at peace, JESUS CHRIST, eternal God and Son of the eternal Father . . . was born of the Virgin Mary in Bethlehem of Judah."

Jesus both personified and preached true and perfect peace. He taught that "all who take the sword will perish by the sword" (Mt 26:52) and admonished, "If any one strikes you on the right cheek, turn to him the other also" (Mt 5:39). Jesus proclaimed peacemakers to be "blessed" and "sons of God" (Mt 5:9). Among his last words to the Apostles before his Passion were, "Peace I leave with you; my peace I give to you" (Jn 14:27). Jesus' life of peace culminated in his peaceful acceptance of death on a cross and his words, "Father, forgive them; for they know not what they do" (Lk 23:34).

Jesus is also the perfection of the wisdom of Solomon. Solomon requested and was granted wisdom. Jesus was born imbued with wisdom. Even as a child, "all who heard him were amazed at his understanding" (Lk 2:47). When the crowds were astonished at his preaching, Jesus specifically compared himself to Solomon, acknowledging Solomon's wisdom but also stating, "Behold, something greater than Solomon is here" (Mt 12:42). Where Solomon was granted wisdom from God, St. Paul points out that Jesus is the "wisdom of God" (1 Cor 1:24).

Lastly, Jesus is the perfection of the Temple built by Solomon. Solomon built a Temple in which God dwelt in the form of a cloud. Jesus is the Temple of God in whom "the whole fulness of deity dwells bodily" (Col 2:9). The Temple of Solomon was destroyed four hundred years later by Nebuchadnezzar. Sixty years thereafter, it was rebuilt and survived for another five hundred years. Standing in the rebuilt Temple, Jesus stated, "Destroy this temple, and in three days I will raise it up" (Jn 2:19). Jesus was crucified, died, and rose three days later, never to die again. Approximately forty years thereafter, the Temple of Solomon was destroyed and remains so today.

Meditation 2: The Second Coming of Christ

As a young man seeking to establish himself as king, we would expect Solomon to ask for military power, riches, or a long reign. Instead, he asked for wisdom. In this, Solomon is a good model for our preparation for the Second Coming of Christ. Wealth, power, success, and prestige are of no eternal value. We will die one day, and none of these things will follow us past the grave. Nor will these things help us when we stand before the throne of God and are called to give an account of our lives. In fact, they may well hinder our entrance into Heaven. Recall the words of Jesus, "It is easier for a camel to go through the eye of a needle than for a rich man to enter the kingdom of heaven" (Mk 10:25).

Power, prestige, wealth, and the like are not bad in themselves if obtained through appropriate means and with an appropriate attitude. Why do we desire these things? If merely to increase comfort and pleasure here on earth, then earth, rather than Heaven, is our focus and our end. If we accept these blessings humbly and thankfully and use them generously for the good of our neighbor, then we store up real treasure in Heaven. Wisdom and knowledge of God's ways are of infinitely greater value to us as they point the way to Heaven.

God assured Solomon, "If you will walk in my ways, keeping my statutes and my commandments, as your father David walked, then I will lengthen your days" (1 Kgs 3:14). On its surface, God appears to be promising Solomon a long physical life in return for his living according to God's Commandments. In fact, Solomon lived only to the age of sixty — not particularly impressive, especially in comparison to many of the Patriarchs such as Abraham (175 years old), Isaac (180 years old), and Moses (120 years old). God was not offering Solomon a long physical life but an eternal life in Heaven. And God offers us the same. How do you view your wealth, power, or prestige?

Meditation 3: The Third Coming of Christ

Solomon asked for wisdom, and it was granted to him. God not only granted him wisdom but riches and honor as well, establishing him as the greatest king of his time. Then God said to him, "And if you will walk in my ways, keeping my statutes and my commandments, as your father David walked, then I will lengthen your days" (1 Kgs 3:14). In this, we learn that Solomon's request was good but, perhaps, not the best.

Solomon was a great king and is lauded throughout many of the books of the Bible. But David is revered above Solomon. Jesus the Messiah is not referred to as "Son of Solomon" but "Son of David." David, not Solomon, is referred to by God as "a man after my heart, who will do all my will" (Acts 13:22; see also 1 Sm 13:14). At the very moment of granting him his request, God challenged Solomon to walk in his ways, as did David.

What elevated David above Solomon? Love. Solomon's great attribute was wisdom. David's was love. David loved Saul, despite

Saul's hatred of him. David loved his son Absalom, even when Absalom usurped his throne and sought to kill him. David danced with reckless abandonment before God's Ark. He composed psalms of his love for God and God's love for us. When confronted with his sins by the prophet Nathan, David immediately admitted his fault and repented.

If we want our Lord to come into our lives today, we must love. Jesus declared the greatest commandments were to love God with our whole heart, mind, soul, and strength and to love our neighbor as ourselves. He admonished us to love each other as he loved us. Jesus asked us to love our enemies and pray for our persecutors. He noted that we would be known as his disciples if we love one another. Jesus assured us that great sins are forgiven those who love greatly. St. Paul remarked that of all the things that survive into Heaven, the greatest is love.

Today, let us welcome Christ into our hearts. Let us ask Christ to increase our love. Let us cry out, "I love you, even when I do not act in love." Let us seek to see Christ in others and love them because Christ is living in them. If our Lord were to say to you, "Ask what I shall give you," what would you ask of him?

DECEMBER 20

Reading: The Birth of John the Baptist Foretold[1]

In the days of Herod, king of Judea, there was a priest named Zechari'ah, of the division of Abi'jah; and he had a wife of the daughters of Aaron, and her name was Elizabeth. And they were both righteous before God, walking in all the commandments and ordinances of the Lord blamelessly. But they had no child, because Elizabeth was barren, and both were advanced in years.

Now while he was serving as priest before God when his division was on duty, according to the custom of the priesthood, it fell to him by lot to enter the temple of the Lord and burn incense. And the whole multitude of the people were praying outside at the hour of incense. And there appeared to him an angel of the Lord standing on the right side of the altar of incense. And Zechari'ah was troubled when he saw him, and fear fell upon him. But the angel said to him, "Do not be afraid, Zechari'ah, for your prayer is heard, and your wife Elizabeth will bear you a son, and you shall call his name John.

And you will have joy and gladness,
And many will rejoice at his birth;
for he will be great before the Lord,
and he shall drink no wine nor strong drink,
and he will be filled with the Holy Spirit,
even from his mother's womb.
And he will turn many of the sons of Israel to the Lord
their God,

---

[1] Luke 1:5–25.

and he will go before him in the spirit and power of Elijah,
to turn the hearts of the fathers to the children,
and the disobedient to the wisdom of the just,
to make ready for the Lord a people prepared."

And Zechariah said to the angel, "How shall I know this? For I am an old man, and my wife is advanced in years." And the angel answered him, "I am Gabriel, who stand in the presence of God; and I was sent to speak to you, and to bring you this good news. And behold, you will be silent and unable to speak until the day that these things come to pass, because you did not believe my words, which will be fulfilled in their time." And the people were waiting for Zechariah, and they wondered at his delay in the temple. And when he came out, he could not speak to them, and they perceived that he had seen a vision in the temple; and he made signs to them and remained mute. And when his time of service was ended, he went to his home.

After these days his wife Elizabeth conceived, and for five months she hid herself, saying, "Thus the Lord has done to me in the days when he looked on me, to take away my reproach among men."

Meditation 1: The First Coming of Christ

John is the direct forerunner of Jesus Christ. He is the last of the biblical figures who point to Jesus. Gabriel's visit and announcement to Zechariah is the foreshadowing of the visit of Gabriel to the Blessed Virgin Mary to announce the birth of the Messiah.

When the angel Gabriel appeared to Zechariah, even before he spoke, Zechariah was both "troubled" and "afraid" (see Lk 1:12). Gabriel's appearance does not, however, evoke either such reaction in Mary. Rather, only after Gabriel addresses her with the words, "Hail, full of grace, the Lord is with you!" (Lk 1:28), is she, in her humility, troubled by the praise heaped on her by this heavenly messenger. To Zechariah, Gabriel announces the almost inconceivable — Elizabeth, who was presumed to be barren, will conceive and bear a son in her old age. To Mary, Gabriel announces the miraculous — she, who is a virgin, will conceive and bear a Son.

Zechariah's son is to be named "John," meaning "God is gracious." Mary's Son is to be named Jesus, meaning "God saves." John would announce the goodness of God that was about to be exhibited par excellence in the coming of the Messiah. Jesus would come to fulfill this announcement and to save God's people. Gabriel revealed to Zechariah that John would go before the Lord and announce his coming, turning people away from sin and preparing their hearts for the coming of the Lord. Gabriel revealed to Mary that Jesus would be called Son of the Most High, sit on the throne of his father David, and reign over the house of Jacob and that there would be no end to his Kingdom.

John points to the priestly and prophetic roles of Jesus. As Zechariah and Elizabeth were of priestly families, John would, by his birthright, be a priest. By his calling, John would be the last prophet before the Messiah. As Mary was a relative of Elizabeth, she presumably was of a priestly family too. Joseph was (and it is likely that Mary was as well) of the lineage of King David. Jesus lived as the perfect prophet of God, calling all to himself. Hence, as a human, Jesus was priest, prophet, and king. As God, however, he is the High Priest, the greatest prophet, and the King of Kings.

Meditation 2: The Second Coming of Christ

The beginning of this passage is evocative of the end times as envisioned in the Book of Revelation (particularly Revelation 8:1–4). It takes place in the Temple of the Lord, where an angel is standing before the altar. There is burning incense, and the prayers of the multitude are rising up before the Lord.

The prophets Joel and Zephaniah refer to the Judgment Day in words that are often translated as "the great and terrible day of the LORD" (Joel 2:31), or sometimes the "great and awesome" day of the Lord. We must, from these words, understand that the Day of Judgment, whether our Particular Judgment at the end of our lives or the end of times, will be truly awesome and overwhelming. While we cannot fully grasp what this moment will be like, we are encouraged to at least ponder Christ's coming to us at the end of our lives and to imagine what our response will be.

In this story, Zechariah is troubled and filled with fear. Yet the angel assures Zechariah that he will soon be filled with joy and gladness. What will fill our hearts when we meet our Lord face to face? Will we be ashamed of how we have lived? Will we fear the Lord's judgment? Or will we humbly place our failures before the throne of God and trust in God's divine mercy? Undoubtedly, we will be awestruck at the grandeur of God, but we must also hope that our fears will melt into joy and gladness in God's presence.

Zechariah walked "in all the commandments and ordinances of the Lord" (Lk 1:60). Yet there was some hardness of his heart that prevented him from accepting the words of God spoken by the angel. He was not yet ready for joy and gladness. He had to be purified in silence for a period of time. But the angel assured him that he would ultimately rejoice. This is a great consolation to us. It may well be that at our death, we are not yet fully ready to receive the joy of Heaven. Rather, we may need to be purified in Purgatory. But we can take heart that, if Purgatory is to be our lot, following this purification, we will eternally rejoice with Zechariah and with the saints and angels in the presence of our Lord.

Imagine yourself on the day that you meet your Lord. What will he say to you? How will you respond?

Meditation 3: The Third Coming of Christ

There are two points highlighted by this passage that are particularly germane to the coming of Christ into our lives today. The first is persistence in prayer. The second is encounter and conversion.

Persistence in prayer. It is a beautiful testament to the faithfulness of Zechariah that, despite the fact that Elizabeth was barren, and despite the fact that they were both advanced in age, the prayer of Zechariah's heart was still to have children. From his response to the angel, it appears that Zechariah did not believe that it was possible. But, on some level, he continued to share his hope with the Lord.

All of us have hopes that we doubt will be realized. We may be childless, suffer from a chronic illness, or have a son or granddaughter who has left the Faith. We cry out to God daily for his intervention. And we wait. The reality is that God hears our prayers. He is ever-mindful of our suffering. For reasons we may not come to understand in this life, our Lord may not choose to answer our prayer in the way we desire. Or, maybe, he will. The important thing is to continue to pray and to continue to trust that God loves us. Every day, we must ask God to enter into our lives and pray that his will be done.

Encounter and conversion. Zechariah encountered God in a way he never expected. He went into the Temple to offer prayers to the Lord, and the Lord sent an angel to speak directly to him. Despite his life of righteousness, Zechariah did not respond well. He responded in fear and doubted the angel's words.

The coming of Christ to each of us daily is all about encounter and conversion. Christ comes to us and calls us to a conversion of heart and mind. It is not often through the proclamation of a heavenly messenger. Rather, it is usually through very mundane means. It may be through the words of Scripture or a challenging homily. It may be through an encounter with a beggar or a test at work. Oftentimes, Christ calls us to grow closer to him through the words of our friends and family.

Every day, Christ reaches out to us personally. He requests admittance into our hearts. He challenges us to change our ways. Then he waits patiently. How will you respond?

DECEMBER 21

Reading: The Annunciation[1]

In the sixth month the angel Gabriel was sent from God to a city
of Galilee named Nazareth, to a virgin betrothed to a man whose
name was Joseph, of the house of David; and the virgin's name
was Mary. And he came to her and said, "Hail, full of grace, the
Lord is with you!" But she was greatly troubled at the saying, and
considered in her mind what sort of greeting this might be. And
the angel said to her, "Do not be afraid, Mary, for you have found
favor with God. And behold, you will conceive in your womb and
bear a son, and you shall call his name Jesus.

> He will be great, and will be called the Son of the Most High;
> and the Lord God will give to him the throne of his
>   father David,
> and he will reign over the house of Jacob for ever;
> and of his kingdom there will be no end."

And Mary said to the angel, "How can this be, since I have no
husband?" And the angel said to her,

> "The Holy Spirit will come upon you,
> and the power of the Most High will overshadow you;
> therefore the child to be born will be called holy,
> the Son of God.

And behold, your kinswoman Elizabeth in her old age has also
conceived a son; and this is the sixth month with her who was
called barren. For with God nothing will be impossible." And
Mary said, "Behold, I am the handmaid of the Lord; let it be to
me according to your word." And the angel departed from her.

[1]   Luke 1:26–38.

123

Meditation 1: The First Coming of Christ

As we draw close to the celebration of Christmas and read the accounts of what happened leading up to our Lord's coming as man, we begin to see the fulfillment of the many Old Testament prophecies regarding the coming of the Messiah. All of salvation history is coming to its pinnacle moment. The long-awaited Savior for whom our ancestors longed is at hand.

The promise of God to Adam and Eve (which we read on the second day of this meditative journey), also referred to as the "protoevangelium" or "first gospel," is fulfilled today. To the serpent (the devil), God said, "I will put enmity between you and the woman, and between your seed and her seed; he shall bruise your head, and you shall bruise his heel" (Gn 3:15). It would be unheard of in Semitic thought to refer to a "woman's seed." Progeny would be referred to as the seed of the man. This prophecy reveals that Jesus would have no biological father and, hence, would be the physical seed only of a woman. Today, we learn that the seed of the New Eve, Mary, will be born to strike the fatal blow against Satan, freeing mankind from the sin of Adam and Eve and opening the gates of Heaven.

Mary, a virgin, is chosen to bear the Christ, fulfilling the prophecy of Isaiah, "Behold, a virgin shall conceive and bear a son, and shall call his name Imman'u-el" (Is 7:14). No one could have fathomed the depth of this prophecy. As amazing as the birth of a son to a virgin, even more amazing is the reality of that Son. "Imman'u-el" means "God is with us." In the birth of Jesus, God came to dwell with us bodily as man, to walk among us, sharing our own human nature.

We previously read of God's promise to David, spoken by the prophet Nathan, "When your days are fulfilled and you lie down with your fathers, I will raise up your offspring after you, who shall come forth from your body, and I will establish his kingdom. He shall build a house for my name, and I will establish the throne of his kingdom forever" (2 Sm 7:12–13). No mere human descendant of David could ever fulfill this prophecy. All kingdoms rise and fall. Only through the eternal kingdom of the God-man Jesus, born into the house of David, could this come to fruition.

Meditation 2: The Second Coming of Christ

A constant theme of salvation history recorded in these readings upon which we have meditated during this month is that of God dwelling with his people. God spoke personally to Abraham, Noah, and Moses, guided them, and made covenants with them and their clans. God promised to be their God, and they his people. God dwelt imperfectly among them in the pillars of fire and cloud, in the meeting tent, in the Ark of the Covenant, in the Ten Commandments, and in the Temple.

In today's reading, God consummates his consistent promises to dwell more intimately with us by becoming Incarnate in the womb of Mary. No words could be truer than those of Gabriel in announcing to Mary, "The Lord is with you!" (Lk 1:28). For, upon her yes, God was with her and in her — the Body, Blood, Soul, and Divinity of the Second Person of the Trinity chose to be contained within her womb. And God would not merely dwell hidden within the womb of Mary but be born and walk among all men: "Therefore the child to be born will be called holy, the Son of God" (Lk 1:35).

As amazing as is the reality of God's intimate dwelling with his people at his Incarnation, his Second Coming will be far more real, personal, and intimate. We read in the Book of Revelation a description of the Second Coming of Christ: "I heard a great voice from the throne saying, 'Behold, the dwelling of God is with men. He will dwell with them, and they shall be his people, and

God himself will be with them; he will wipe away every tear from their eyes, and death shall be no more'" (Rev 21:3–4).

Comparing Christ's dwelling with us now to that at his Second Coming, St. Paul states, "Now we see in a mirror dimly, but then face to face. Now I know in part; then I shall understand fully, even as I have been fully understood" (1 Cor 13:12). As you look forward this year to celebrating the coming of Christ as man, can you allow your mind to soar for a moment, envisioning the eternal celebration of Christ's coming to you personally at the end of your life?

Meditation 3: The Third Coming of Christ

Contained in this passage is perhaps the most sublime example of how we are to respond to God's presence in our daily lives: "And Mary said, 'Behold, I am the handmaid of the Lord; let it be to me according to your word'" (Lk 1:38).

God is intimately present in every moment of our lives. He is present in our joys and in our sorrows. He is present in our accomplishments and in the challenges facing us. Sometimes, we can see the will of God. Sometimes, we know exactly what he is asking of us. More often, God seems distant and quiet. Regardless, our response should be the same. It should be that of Mary — "Fiat!" "Yes!" "Thy will be done!"

Mary must have been overwhelmed. She could not fathom how the words of the angel were to be fulfilled. She did not know how Joseph and the people around her would react to her pregnancy. How would she raise the Son of God? Yet none of these concerns, nor any fear she had, prevented her from saying, "Yes, Lord, let whatever you will happen to me."

As we draw close to Christmas, let us find some time to sit quietly and speak to God. Let us ask him to draw our hearts closer to him. Let us ask him to reveal his will for us and to give us the strength to bend our will to his. Regardless of God's response, are you willing to say from the very depth of your soul, "Let all things in my life be according to your word."

DECEMBER 22

Reading: The Visitation[1]

In those days Mary arose and went with haste into the hill country, to a city of Judah, and she entered the house of Zechari'ah and greeted Elizabeth. And when Elizabeth heard the greeting of Mary, the child leaped in her womb; and Elizabeth was filled with the Holy Spirit and she exclaimed with a loud cry, "Blessed are you among women, and blessed is the fruit of your womb! And why is this granted me, that the mother of my Lord should come to me? For behold, when the voice of your greeting came to my ears, the child in my womb leaped for joy. And blessed is she who believed that there would be a fulfilment of what was spoken to her from the Lord." And Mary said,

"My soul magnifies the Lord,
and my spirit rejoices in God my Savior,
for he has regarded the low estate of his handmaiden.
For behold, henceforth all generations will call me blessed;
for he who is mighty has done great things for me,
and holy is his name.
And his mercy is on those who fear him
from generation to generation.
He has shown strength with his arm,
he has scattered the proud in the imagination of their hearts,
he has put down the mighty from their thrones,
and exalted those of low degree;
he has filled the hungry with good things,

[1] Luke 1:39–56.

and the rich he has sent empty away.

He has helped his servant Israel,

in remembrance of his mercy,

as he spoke to our fathers,

to Abraham and to his posterity for ever."

And Mary remained with her about three months, and returned to her home.

Meditation 1: The First Coming of Christ

In this passage, the fulfillment of the predictions of the Messiah continues to unfold, particularly in reference to David as a "type" or precursor to Christ.

On December 19, we read how David "arose and went" to the hill country to meet God, to encounter the original Ark of God (which contained symbols of God's power — manna, Aaron's rod that budded, and the tablets inscribed with the Ten Commandments). Today, we read of God journeying to the hill country to meet man. Mary, the New Ark of God (for within her resided not mere symbols of God but God Incarnate), "arose and went" (Lk 1:39) to the hill country to meet Elizabeth. David entered the house of Abina'adab, who was a priest. Mary entered the house of Zechariah, who was a priest. As David brought the Ark from the house of Abina'dab to the city of David, the Ark stayed in the house of O'bed-e'dom (also a priest) for three months. Mary, the New Ark, stayed in the house of Zechariah for three months. In the presence of the Ark, David leaped for joy. In the presence of Christ in the womb of Mary, John leaped for joy in the womb of Elizabeth.

As David was raised up from humble beginnings, Mary points out her low estate. David would be called "King." Mary would be called "blessed among woman," and Jesus would be called "Son of God." Mary remarks that God "has put down the mighty from their thrones, and exalted those of low degree" (Lk 1:52). This is especially seen in the lives of David and his successors. David went from being the youngest child and a shepherd to reigning as King of Israel. David and his heirs generally had rocky, short-lived reigns (David even lost his throne for a period of time to his son Absalom's treachery). Yet David was promised that his kingdom would last forever and his heir would sit on a throne forever. This is fulfilled in Christ, who is the King of Kings and whose reign will never end.

Meditation 2: The Second Coming of Christ

As we have acknowledged many times during our meditations on the Second Coming, we cannot merit entry into Heaven. Only God's mercy will open the gates for us. This passage underscores that humility is the key to obtaining everlasting life. It is humility that most directly leads to mercy.

Here we see humility modeled. Elizabeth is the elder and of a priestly family. Mary is the younger and married to a tradesman. Yet Elizabeth is overwhelmed that Mary would condescend to visit her. In response, Mary, who is blessed among women (see Lk 1:42) and whom all generations will call blessed (see Lk 1:48), deflects all praise and honor from herself and directs it to the Lord. Mary accounts herself lowly and instead "magnifies the Lord" (Lk 1:46).

Mary proclaims the mercy of the Lord, recognizing that God "has put down the mighty from their thrones, and exalted those of low degree; he has filled the hungry with good things, and the rich he has sent empty away" (Lk 1:52–53). Like the Beatitudes, these statements must not be read narrowly. Our position in life and our finances will not, in themselves, determine whether or not we will receive the merciful gift of Heaven. Rather, it is our disposition towards our possessions and position that will be determinative.

We must remain humble and hungry for God, regardless of what we have or do not have.

Mary remarks that God "has scattered the proud in the imagination of their hearts" (Lk 1:51) and "helped his servant Israel, in remembrance of his mercy" (Lk 1:54). The proud imagine that they do not need God. The humble see themselves as lowly servants of God. Hence, the proud deny God's saving power, and the humble beg for it. If we wish to receive mercy at the Second Coming, we must, as St. Paul points out, seek to imitate the humility of Christ, "who, though he was in the form of God, did not count equality with God a thing to be grasped, but emptied himself, taking the form of a servant, being born in the likeness of men. And being found in human form he humbled himself and became obedient unto death" (Phil 2:6–8). Where are you lacking in humility? How might you shift your focus away from yourself and toward God?

Meditation 3: The Third Coming of Christ

After the angel Gabriel's announcement that she would conceive and bear the Son of God, Mary did not go into seclusion and focus on herself and what was about to happen. Rather, she "went with haste" (Lk 1:39) to attend to Elizabeth in her pregnancy. Mary's spirit rejoiced in God, and her soul magnified the Lord (see Lk 1:46–47). Likewise, in the presence of God, hidden in the womb of Mary, Elizabeth was filled with joy. She focused not on her own pregnancy but "exclaimed with a loud cry" (Lk 1:42) praises of Mary and of God. Even John, not yet born, leaped in her womb.

Every day, our Lord approaches us in sometimes big and sometimes small ways. Every day is an opportunity to respond to our Lord's invitation to accept his salvation, to know him better, and to love him more dearly. God desires us to grow more closely to him every day, but he will not force this relationship. He approaches. He knocks upon the door of our hearts. But we must respond. We must open the door and bid him enter.

The moment of time depicted in this passage is a seminal moment. It is the meeting of the Mother of the Messiah with the mother of the forerunner — he who would be the last to prepare the way for the coming of the Christ. Mary, Elizabeth, and John each encountered Christ and responded joyfully. We constantly encounter Christ and are given the opportunity to respond similarly. God desires us to respond not with timidity but with a reckless love, to cry out with tears in our eyes and our heart pounding, "Yes, Lord! I love you, Lord! I will go where you lead!" How do you respond to God's presence in your life?

DECEMBER 23

Reading: The Birth of John[1]

Now the time came for Elizabeth to be delivered, and she gave birth to a son. And her neighbors and kinsfolk heard that the Lord had shown great mercy to her, and they rejoiced with her. And on the eighth day they came to circumcise the child; and they would have named him Zechari'ah after his father, but his mother said, "Not so; he shall be called John." And they said to her, "None of your kindred is called by this name." And they made signs to his father, inquiring what he would have him called. And he asked for a writing tablet, and wrote, "His name is John." And they all marveled. And immediately his mouth was opened and his tongue loosed, and he spoke, blessing God. And fear came on all their neighbors. And all these things were talked about through all the hill country of Judea; and all who heard them laid them up in their hearts, saying, "What then will this child be?" For the hand of the Lord was with him.

And his father Zechari'ah was filled with the Holy Spirit, and prophesied, saying,

"Blessed be the Lord God of Israel,

for he has visited and redeemed his people,

and has raised up a horn of salvation for us in the house of his servant David,

as he spoke by the mouth of his holy prophets from of old,

that we should be saved from our enemies,

and from the hand of all who hate us;

---

[1] Luke 1:57–80.

> to perform the mercy promised to our fathers,
> and to remember his holy covenant,
> the oath which he swore to our father Abraham, to grant us
> that we, being delivered from the hand of our enemies,
> might serve him without fear,
> in holiness and righteousness before him all the days of
>   our life.
> And you, child, will be called the prophet of the Most High;
> for you will go before the Lord to prepare his ways,
> to give knowledge of salvation to his people
> in the forgiveness of their sins,
> through the tender mercy of our God,
> when the day shall dawn upon us from on high
> to give light to those who sit in darkness and in the shadow
>   of death,
> to guide our feet into the way of peace."

And the child grew and became strong in spirit, and he was in the wilderness till the day of his manifestation to Israel.

Meditation 1: The First Coming of Christ

Zechariah announced that the fulfillment of the prophecies concerning the coming of the Messiah was at hand. The Messiah to be born of the house of David was already Incarnate, hidden in the womb of Mary. He had come to save God's people. However, God's people were in for a surprise — the Messiah was not exactly who they had expected.

The Israelites generally anticipated the coming of a human leader who would save them from the earthly tyranny of political oppressors (currently the Romans). They believed that they would be set free to live abundantly on earth and worship God freely according to the Law of Moses.

Zechariah revealed that "the Lord . . . has visited . . . his people" (Lk 1:68). The Messiah was not merely a great prophet or king. Rather, the Messiah was the Lord himself, the Son of God, the second Person of the Holy Trinity. God did not send a representative as he did throughout salvation history but came himself to accomplish the work of salvation.

Zechariah revealed that God would not merely save the people from earthly oppression. Rather, as his son John would announce to all, the Messiah would bring "salvation to his people in the forgiveness of their sins" (Lk 1:77). The Messiah would not free the people from earthly shackles but redeem mankind from the sin of Adam, from all personal sin, and from the eternal death that results from sin. The Messiah would not come to make sure a small group of people could worship freely according to the imperfect prescriptions given to Moses. Rather, all of the true children of Abraham (children not merely by blood but children because of their faith in the God of Abraham — that is, every one of us) would be given the ability to worship in Spirit and in truth in the perfect prescriptions of Jesus. The Messiah would, by his death and Resurrection, reveal that the blessings to be poured out by God through the Messiah would not be limited to our lives here on earth but would be bestowed upon us for all eternity.

Meditation 2: The Second Coming of Christ

Despite the revelation that Christ has come as Savior, to a great extent, we remain as "those who sit in darkness and the shadow of death" (Lk 1:79). We still possess mortal bodies subject to the corruption and death imposed upon us by the sin of Adam and Eve. Our intellect is still darkened. As St. Paul reminds us, "our knowledge is imperfect" and "now we see in a mirror dimly" (1 Cor 13:9, 12). Accordingly, we cannot fathom the Second Coming of Christ. But, when he comes again, the imperfect will give way to the perfect, we will see God face to face, and we will understand fully (see 1 Cor 13:9, 12).

It is a normal human emotion to fear death because, despite our faith, there is always some doubt. Even if we have little doubt of the truth of Heaven, we may still fear God's judgment. Even if that fear is small, there often remains a general fear of the unknown. To these fears and doubts, Zechariah assures us that the Day of Judgment will be a day on which God will show his "tender mercy" (Lk 1:78) in the forgiveness of our sins (see Lk 1:79). It will be a day of joy, marked by the triumphant sound of the horn of God's salvation. On that day, we will forever be saved from the hands of our enemies — sin, temptation, and fear. We will be transformed — holy and righteous in the sight of God — and we will forever walk in the way of peace. St. Paul echoes this sentiment, reminding us that "no eye has seen, nor ear hear heard, nor heart conceived, what God has prepared for those who love him" (1 Cor 2:9).

Today, just one day away from the celebration of the birth of Christ, let us juxtapose the First Coming of Christ against his Second Coming. The image of the First Coming brings us so much peace and joy — the unfathomable personal love of God shown by his setting aside his glory to become man, the tenderness of the Child in the arms of the Blessed Mother, the peacefulness of the night in which the meek and the great meet together to worship at the stable, and the glory of the heavenly sign and the announcement of angelic beings. If even the mere shadows of this First Coming have the power to fill us with joy, how unfathomably greater will be the joy of the Second Coming! Can you imagine Christ coming to you at the end of your life peacefully, lovingly, and joyfully?

Meditation 3: The Third Coming of Christ

The nature of the First Coming of Christ, as announced by Zechariah, is particularly instructive for how we should receive Christ daily into our lives as Savior. Zechariah promised that the Messiah would save us "from our enemies, and from the hand of all who hate us" (Lk 1:71). Yet Jesus would not, as expected by many, free the Israelites from the earthly rulers that oppressed them. We must then look to Jesus' own words for help in understanding what this means. "Do not fear those who kill the body but cannot kill the soul; rather fear him who can destroy both soul and body in hell" (Mt 10:28). Jesus assured us that our true enemy here on earth is not any political leader, terrorist group, or criminal element. Our true enemy is the devil and sin. These are the enemies Jesus came to save us from.

In his First Coming, our Lord won for us eternal salvation through his life, death, and Resurrection. Because of this, we can take to heart the words of Zechariah and "serve him without fear" (Lk 1:74), knowing that Heaven is ours. But, as God has given us free will, we may choose to accept or reject this gift of salvation. In fact, we are sinners and sin every day. We must not, however, despair, for we have been given "knowledge of salvation" by the "forgiveness of [our] sins" (Lk 1:77). Every day, God pours out mercy upon us. He is available in the Sacraments of Reconciliation and the Eucharist. Through these sacraments of love and mercy, our Lord forgives sins and offers eternal life. We must, therefore, frequently avail ourselves of these sacraments.

Even with the revelation that the Messiah has already come and won our salvation, we remain to a certain extent "in darkness and in the shadow of death" (Lk 1:79). Our intellect is clouded. Our will is weak. We are subject to pain and death. And we feel lost. But our Lord promises to be the light in the darkness and to guide us. Because of our weakness and sin, we are prone to shame and despair. But our Lord promises to come not with harsh judgment but with "tender mercy" (Lk 1:78). In answer to our anxiety, our Lord promises to lead us to peace.

Are you willing to embrace Christ's mercy? Will you accept the salvation he won for you? Will you walk in his light and follow in his way of peace? Will you, like John, share this Good News of Christ's mercy and salvation with others?

DECEMBER 24

Reading: The Birth of Jesus[1]

In those days a decree went out from Caesar Augustus that all
the world should be enrolled. This was the first enrollment, when
Quirinıus was governor of Syria. And all went to be enrolled,
each to his own city. And Joseph also went up from Galilee, from
the city of Nazareth, to Judea, to the city of David, which is called
Bethlehem, because he was of the house and lineage of David,
to be enrolled with Mary his betrothed, who was with child. And
while they were there, the time came for her to be delivered. And
she gave birth to her first-born son and wrapped him in swaddling
cloths, and laid him in a manger, because there was no place for
them in the inn.

And in that region there were shepherds out in the field, keeping watch over their flock by night. And an angel of the Lord
appeared to them, and the glory of the Lord shone around them,
and they were filled with fear. And the angel said to them, "Be not
afraid; for behold, I bring you good news of a great joy which will
come to all the people; for to you is born this day in the city of
David a Savior, who is Christ the Lord. And this will be a sign for
you: you will find a baby wrapped in swaddling cloths and lying in
a manger." And suddenly there was with the angel a multitude of
the heavenly host praising God and saying,

"Glory to God in the highest,
and on earth peace among men with whom he is pleased!"

[1] Luke 2:1–20.

When the angels went away from them into heaven, the shepherds said to one another, "Let us go over to Bethlehem and see this thing that has happened, which the Lord has made known to us." And they went with haste, and found Mary and Joseph, and the baby lying in a manger. And when they saw it they made known the saying which had been told them concerning this child; and all who heard it wondered at what the shepherds told them. But Mary kept all these things, pondering them in her heart. And the shepherds returned, glorifying and praising God for all they had heard and seen, as it had been told them.

Meditation 1: The First Coming of Christ

Over the last twenty-three days, we have prayerfully entered into salvation history and embraced the longing of mankind for the coming of the Messiah that began with the first sin of Adam and Eve at the dawn of creation. Today, the pinnacle of physical creation is celebrated. God has come as man. A "New Adam" is born who will reverse the effects of the sin of the first Adam. Today, the promise of salvation made by God to Adam and Eve immediately after their Fall is realized — the "seed of Eve" has come to strike a fatal blow to the devil (and sin itself). [See Meditation 1 for December 2.]

Today, Jesus Christ the Messiah is born in fulfillment of the prophecies made by patriarchs and prophets over the two thousand years preceding his birth. Jesus is born in Bethlehem, the "city of David." This fulfills the words of the Prophet Micah, "But you, O Bethlehem Eph'ratah, who are little to be among the clans of Judah, from you shall come forth for me one who is to be ruler in Israel, whose origin is from of old, from ancient days" (Mi 5:2). Jesus is born of the house and lineage of David as prophesied by Samuel, Isaiah, and Jeremiah. Isaiah prophesied that the messiah would be a "shoot from the stump of Jesse," David's father (Is 11:1). Samuel revealed that it would not be David but an heir of David who would be the eternal king and true son of God: "When your days are fulfilled and you lie down with your fathers, I will raise up your offspring after you, who shall come forth from your body, and I will establish his kingdom. He shall build a house for my name, and I will establish the throne of his kingdom forever. I will be his father, and he shall be my son" (2 Sm 7:12–14). Jeremiah confirms this: "Behold, the days are coming, says the LORD, when I will raise up for David a righteous Branch, and he shall reign as king and ... Judah will be saved" (Jer 23:5–6).

Jesus is born of the Virgin Mary in fulfillment of the prophecy of Isaiah to King Ahaz, "Behold, a virgin shall conceive and bear a son, and shall call his name Imman'u-el" (Is 7:14). The announcement by the angels of this unexpected birth was foreshadowed by the visit of heavenly messengers to Abraham to announce the impending birth of a son to Abraham and Sarah despite their old age (see Gn 18:2–10). That the Messiah would be born in lowly estate, found in a manger, and visited by shepherds fulfill the prophecy of Isaiah that the Messiah would be like a young plant that would grow out of dry soil and would have nothing remarkable about him that we would look at him (see Is 53:2).

For the past twenty-three days, we have joined in the longing of all creation for the coming of the King of Kings and Lord of Lords — he who would defeat sin and open the gates of Heaven to us. Today, we celebrate that this wait is over. Christ has come!

Meditation 2: The Second Coming of Christ

It may seem counterintuitive to focus on the Second Coming of Christ on the eve of his First Coming. Why would we focus on an event ushered in by our death at the time we celebrate birth? It is appropriate and useful to so meditate because the unavoidable consequence of birth is death and because death ushers in a new and glorious rebirth.

Our Lord was wrapped in "swaddling clothes" (Lk 2:7). The infinite God lowered himself to become a little, helpless baby, tightly bound and laid in a manger. In doing so, he foreshadowed the ultimate self-abnegation when he, the Lord of life, would accept death, be bound in a shroud, and laid in a tomb. But neither the manger nor the tomb would constrain the will of God. Christ's birth would end in death, but his death would result in new life — for all of us.

Today, the angels speak to each of us, "Be not afraid; for behold, I bring you good news!" (Lk 2:10). Today, a child has been born who is the promised Savior and Christ. Today, because of his birth, death will be vanquished. Today, death dies and, through a new birth, life lives forever. Today, our new and glorious tomorrow is made available for us.

Mary quietly pondered all that was happening and would so quietly ponder all of the trials and glories of her Son. Mary pondered so as to come to understand the will of God and the meaning of these things. Let us join with Mary today in her pondering. Let us not merely focus on a joyful event that took place two thousand years ago but on its import for us personally and for all of creation for all eternity.

As you ponder the coming of Christ at Christmas, can you look forward to Christ's death and Resurrection? In the same way, can you set aside any fear you might have of your own death in the sure knowledge that you were not made for death but for eternal life with Christ?

Meditation 3: The Third Coming of Christ

Today, Christ comes to us as he did to the shepherds on that holy night two thousand years ago. Let us welcome him into our hearts as they did and act according to their example.

The shepherds were "keeping watch over their flock by night" (Lk 2:8). Every moment our Lord comes to us right where we are. Let us be prepared for his coming. Let us "keep watch." Let us be ready. Let us look for his coming. Let us keep watch "over our flock." Let us take care of those people and those matters entrusted to us by God. Let us be especially mindful to keep watch over our own souls. Let us not neglect our duty to remain vigilant even when it is "night" — when we are tired, discouraged, or do not feel God's presence in our life. Even if we are isolated, in the wilderness, and in darkness, Christ will surely come!

We must be open to the Word of God. We must listen and react. God speaks to us in no less of a real way through Scripture than he did to the shepherds through the words of angels. The angels brought "good news" of a seminal event in salvation history. Contained in the Bible is the entirety of the "Good News," from creation to the Incarnation to the Resurrection and beyond. Just as it did to the shepherds, the words of God can cause us momentary fear. But we must, like the shepherds, trust in God's words and in his love for us and go where he asks.

Today is Christmas. It is a wonderful day of celebration to be savored. But we cannot tarry. Rather, like the shepherds, we must go "in haste" (Lk 2:16) to where we are sent. God comes to us today and sends us forth on a journey. We must, as did the shepherds, make known to others what has happened. We must share the Good News: God loves us so much that he became man to suffer and die for our sins, to save us from death, to remove all that separates us from God, to wipe away every tear, and to give us eternal peace and joy with him in Heaven. Let us today, along with the shepherds, go forth "glorifying and praising God" (Lk 2:20) through both our lives and our words!

Where is God sending you? With whom does God ask you to share his Good News?

Glory to God in the highest,
and on earth peace among men with whom he is pleased!
— *Luke 2:14*